M000286394

I'd Rather Have A Root Canal Than Do Cold Calling!

Third Edition

I'd Rather Have A Root Canal Than Do Cold Calling!

Third Edition

Shawn A. Greene

SuccessWorks Publishing

El Sobrante, California

I'D RATHER HAVE A ROOT CANAL
THAN DO COLD CALLING!

Copyright 2016 Shawn A. Davis (writing as Shawn A. Greene).
All rights reserved. No part of this work may be reproduced or transmitted
in any form or by any means, electronic or mechanical, including photocopying,
scanning, recording, faxing, emailing, posting online or by any information storage
and retrieval system without express prior permission by Shawn A. Davis.
Unauthorized use, reproduction or distribution of the material contained in this work
is a violation of federal law and punishable by civil and criminal penalty.

Training programs covering the same skills and content also copyrighted
with all rights reserved. No part of this work may be used for training
without express prior permission by Shawn A. Davis (Shawn A. Greene).

For more information or to request permission:
use the contact page on SavageAndGreene.com

ISBN 978-0-9702731-0-9

This edition has an ebook version available through many fine purveyors

Second Edition: Copyright 2008
ISBN 978-0-9702731-3-0

First Edition: Copyright 1999
ISBN 0-9702731-9-3

Harriet the Spy was written by Louise Fitzhugh

"Mom," I asked, "do you think I could be a real writer some day?"

"Yes," you replied

This is for you, Momma Savage

Thank you for reading *Harriet the Spy* to me, chapter by chapter

Thank you for taking my question seriously

and for giving me my own notebook with the special pen holder

(two, because I lost the first one)

I miss you every single day

The Root Canal Effect: Then and Now

I WAS ABOUT to deliver my first telemarketing workshop. The room was set, flipcharts were up and spiffy binders were ready to hand out.

Students slowly trickled in, grabbing coffee and a croissant (the hot training snack at the time) before sitting down. They looked glum. Almost everyone who was not eating sat with their arms crossed. There was an air of something close to hostility and despair wafting up from more than a few people. Just one or two returned my smile.

That may have been my first telemarketing class but it wasn't the first time I needed to find out what was going on. I abandoned the planned icebreaker and asked the group how they felt about being in class—and the new requirement to make outbound calls.

The first student said, "My boss made me come."

The second mumbled, "It's my job now, whether I want to or not."

The third rolled his eyes and said, "You wanna know how I feel about doing cold calling? I'd rather have a root canal!"

That was 1993. All these years later, that's still the best description of how most people feel about making cold calls. Then and now, people worry about what cold calling will do to their image. After all, only rookies and losers should have to make cold calls, right? They also dread the frustration, repetition, awkwardness and rejection.

Even people who grew up after Do Not Call laws were implemented would rather have a root canal than pick up the phone and call a bunch of strangers. Most have little idea why those laws were put in place but they still get the message that making cold calls is somehow bad.

Warm is supposedly better...

The more people grew to hate making cold calls, the more experts said other marketing tools were better. Back in 1993, networking and referrals were supposedly better. (Never mind we picked up the phone to develop our network and reach referred prospects, and still do.)

For a while, mailing was supposed to be better. Then came email, web-based stuff, and the current anything-but-cold-calling darlings: social media and social networking.

In many cases, the idea is not to avoid the phone altogether. Instead, we're supposed to "warm" calls up by doing things like completing research so we can customize each call, or tie our call to something mailed earlier.

Sure, we still call prospects but since it's not "cold" we should feel better and get better results. If we don't...well, that must mean we're doing something wrong. Right? Wrong again.

...except it's not

This book is not going to teach you a fantastic way to warm calls up because warming calls up does not work.

The things people do to try to "warm" calls up rarely pay off. All of that researching and customizing and sending does not improve calling results and, in fact, often backfires.

For example, many callers like to mail or email something in advance. But when prospects have not read that item—and most have not—the caller's plan for answering questions and discussing things falls apart.

In addition, lots of people (about 30%) feel more nervous about making supposed "warm" calls than they do calling strangers out of the blue. For example, they feel more anxious about calling clients and prospects to whom they've been referred. Why? The stakes feel higher, that's why. And if you have ever been relieved to get a customer's voicemail you've had a taste of what this feels like.

Finally, no matter how warm a call may start out, if you don't handle it well it can get awfully cold awfully quickly.

For all those reasons, it's far better to get comfortable and competent with cold calls—that way you've got it all covered.

What actually works

This book teaches you to use a consultative model for cold calling that is highly effective on both ends of the phone line. You'll also learn what is truth and what is myth, so you'll have sound expectations and guidelines.

Those effective models and realistic expectations give you the tools for much greater success and much less frustration.

There's one more thing you'll need—practice—and I'm not going to fudge the reality here. When you first move forward with consultative calling it may still feel uncomfortable for a little while. That's why this book includes tips for getting through that learning curve.

The good news is it won't take too long for those actions to sink into your brain and gut. You'll not only have much greater success, you'll feel much better, too. Let's get started!

Understanding the Root Canal Effect

THE LIST OF REASONS why people do not want to make cold calls is short but powerful.

People worry prospects won't like getting cold calls, and that their dislike will lead to dismissal of the reason for the call and even personal rejection of the caller.

People worry cold calls project an unprofessional image. They also worry prospects will think they must not be any good at their job. What's more, many worry this is true—that if they *really* had their act together then they wouldn't have to make cold calls.

People also find telemarketing a wee bit frustrating. The things they do don't work well, making the tedious aspects all the more onerous.

All of the above adds up, and those concerns exist even when people have not actually made cold calls. Whether you see those reasons as fear, reluctance or just being realistic, you have to understand where the concerns come from before you can fix them.

So what causes the root canal effect? Three things:

- Direct experience in receiving annoying calls
- Lack of experience with a positive model
- Flawed expectations driven by mythology

I'll start with how experience—or lack of it—affects us as we make calls.

Receiving calls affects making them

If you're old enough to remember the pre-Do-Not-Call law era, you probably received the kind of call that drives most people bananas. (You may even have your phone numbers on the Do Not Call list, which says something all by itself.) Here's what bugs most people:

Right off the bat, we're irritated because the call interrupts what we're doing. More specifically, the caller doesn't care they have interrupted us.

The caller goes on and on and on... They eventually get to the point but we're mighty annoyed in the meantime.

They don't say the full or real reason for the call. We know why they're calling (it's not just to thank us or to introduce themselves) and we wish they would just say that. Instead, they insult our intelligence and waste our time.

Calls that make it sound as if we *should* want what they are selling irritate us, too. Same goes when callers assume we or our business will benefit from what they're offering.

Many callers are downright pushy and ignore our "no" multiple times. It seems like they care most about getting paid for making a sale or getting a contribution.

We don't like it when it sounds like the caller is reading from a script. That whole canned thing rubs us the wrong way.

Last but not least, we don't like calls that are slightly manipulative or invasive.

Not receiving calls affects making them

If you're young enough to have grown up with Do Not Call laws and texting, your impression of using the phone may be even more jaded.

You may have little experience with receiving or making special phone calls; such as on someone's birthday. You may never have spent hours talking with your best buddy on the phone (as opposed to texting).

You may not have seen adults in your life happily conduct business on the phone, as opposed to rolling their eyes and letting calls go to the machine (when there were answering machines). It may also be hard to imagine callers on the other end of the line behaving professionally.

Without a strong positive model, the negative aspects stand out all the more. Concern about rudely interrupting prospects may be particularly high. Having grown up with texting, there's something that seems downright invasive about calling—and that's true.

There is indeed something invasive about the phone. This deserves a deeper look because it's also what makes the phone such a powerful tool.

Power to invade, power to connect

The phone is a terrific way to connect. That voice-to-voice experience is second only to talking in person. The other side of this coin is the phone's capacity to invade.

When the phone rings it has a slightly invasive quality to it—all by itself.

When there is a stranger on the other end of the line, the sense of invasion gets a tiny bit higher. This is an automatic response because it's part of our survival mechanisms.

If that stranger asks us questions our sense of invasion nudges higher still. This applies to personal questions like, "Are you a homeowner?" Ditto for business questions such as, "Do you have more than 25 employees?" And it's true for polite inquiries like the one at the top of everyone's list of annoying things callers say: the question, "How are you?"

Most of us push back against these forms of invasion. We also push back when callers use an assumptive approach and the rest of the annoying techniques.

Who wants to act like that?

All of that brings us back to how experience in receiving annoying calls hurts us as much as lack of a positive model.

Picture yourself preparing for cold calls. You've got your list and script ready. There's a fresh cup of coffee in front of you. You've fluffed up the foam pad on your headset a few times. You take a deep breath, reach for the phone...and here is the image that leaps to mind:

You're going to interrupt people, which will annoy them. You're going to be pushy, assumptive, maybe even slightly manipulative—if you can pull it off—and you're going to sound like some kind of android.

Oh, goodie! No wonder you don't want to make cold calls. You know prospects won't respond well and that's probably not the way you normally handle business, either.

The trouble is, most people accidentally copy the same type of call they themselves reject. They copy it because that irritating, invasive, boring, assumptive model is the only one they know or were taught.

Fortunately, those annoyances aren't the only things you and your prospects have in common. You also have the same preferences, and applying those preferences is a big part of what makes consultative calling so effective.

So drop that and do this

We know what drives our prospects crazy. It's the same stuff that drives us crazy, which means we can avoid it.

One of the things prospects find annoying is being interrupted. Unfortunately, we can't avoid interrupting people, even if all they're doing is organizing paperclips or washing dishes. However, we can show respect for their time by asking permission to essentially continue the interruption, and continuing only if we get permission. This also helps us focus our efforts on prospects who do indeed have time and inclination to hear us out.

We can avoid blabbing on and on by being direct and upfront about the reason for our call. This also avoids an annoying unstated agenda. As a bonus, being direct and upfront projects a confident, professional image.

To avoid an assumptive approach, we can make it clear we are <u>looking</u> for wants, needs and interests. This benefits us, too, by keeping us grounded in reality and preventing frustration.

Instead of asking prospects nosy yet useless questions like "When was the last time you had your portfolio reviewed?" or "How often does your broker shop for better rates?" we can provide information <u>to</u> them. We can proactively talk about our products, our services, our experience and so on. This not only avoids invading their space and prompting push-back, it often helps spark interest where there was none before.

As for avoiding being pushy, that may seem like a no-brainer but it often requires a change in mindset. Here's why:

People who use telemarketing tend to be in jobs which involve problem-solving, and problem-solvers tend to be very attracted to challenges. That normally positive quality translates to being pushy when cold calling. To avoid this, we need to learn to be more attracted to opportunities and to let the big juicy challenges go (for the moment).

The last item to cover is how to avoid sounding canned or overly-scripted. The secret is not about calling without a script—a good script acts as a guide, which keeps us on track and makes calling easier. The secret is to use scripts that sound just like we normally talk. That not only sounds much better, it feels better, too.

The art of consultative style calls

The above provides an overview of what makes calls "consultative." In a nutshell, consultative calls:

- Are direct and to the point about the reason for the call.
- Show respect for each prospect's time and intelligence by being direct and using permission.
- Show respect for each prospect's wants, needs, and interests by using a consultative (not assumptive) approach.
- Go at the prospect's pace.

Next

You may have noticed I didn't say much about flawed expectations and avoiding trying to manipulate those on the other end of the phone line. Maybe you think the latter is no big deal because you're not that kind of caller, anyway.

Well, many callers attempt to manipulate others without realizing that's what they're doing. These attempts, which snowball into frustration and poor results, are often based on ideas about how cold calling is "supposed" to work. Time to bust more myths and set fundamental expectations so you can avoid that trap.

Myth vs. Reality

TELEMARKETING COMES WITH a solid set of myths, many of which are responsible for its negative baggage. These myths also create weird expectations about what you can or "should" be able to do when cold calling. Those unrealistic expectations are major generators of frustration and poor results.

It's important to know what is true and what is not. It's also important to know what you can realistically expect and accomplish. I'll start covering all of that here and then expand and reinforce throughout the book.

Let's start with a basic orientation. You are not selling. You are marketing—telemarketing.

"Marketing" is the stuff we do to gain prospects' attention and regain customers' attention.

Marketing tools include mail, email, networking, canvassing, advertising, web stuff, public speaking, and the telephone. Prospecting is marketing, too, and refers to the more direct marketing tools like telemarketing and canvassing (door to door).

"Selling" begins once you and the prospect have agreed to discuss and examine the fit between what you offer and what they want and need. You're not selling unless and until you have that agreement.

If you don't have agreement that doesn't mean you're stuck or wasting your time. There are things you can do to further the business relationship—you're just doing that within the marketing context.

Draw a line based on agreement

Use the delineator of agreement to draw a mental line between marketing (or prospecting) and selling. That line will help you focus on where you are. We tend to do better when we're focused.

That mental line also guides appropriate expectations, which helps prevent frustration on your end. The line between prospecting and selling also helps prevent us from trying to get prospects to do things they simply won't usually do.

Using agreement as the line is important because the best way to generate agreement is to ask for it. In this case, you're going to ask for a sales conversation. Making that request in a clear and direct manner is a best practice. Here's why:

When the prospect says yes, both parties are on the same page in terms of why you're meeting, talking more, etc. This means you've set a solid foundation for that sales conversation.

When the prospect says no, you know you are still marketing. This orients what you do next and how you feel about that prospect.

Why use the phone?

Before tackling seven fundamental myths, I want to emphasize I'm not saying telemarketing is the one and only best marketing tool around. Most of us need more than one marketing tool in use for greatest success and the phone is an excellent tool to include in the mix.

The phone is a great marketing tool because it leverages a personal touch. It's ideal for projecting our personality, developing rapport, and building relationships when we can't meet in person.

The phone tends to generate results more quickly than most other marketing tools. It's perfect when you want to build your pipeline as fast as possible.

Telemarketing's relative speed also means you don't need momentum for good results. You can put calling aside when you are busy delivering products or services, and then pick it back up when you need to find the next project or new customers.

You don't need special knowledge to use the phone. You don't need to know how to write great marketing copy or how to make search engines love your website. In fact, chances are pretty high you already have the basic skills.

The phone is one of the least expensive marketing tools to use. Best of all, it has a high response rate.

Myth #1: Calling has a low response rate

Part of this myth is based on confusion over what "response rate" means. To clear things up, let's go back to the original response rate, back when old-style mail was a common and very effective marketing tool.

The process started with sending letters to prospects, along with a postage-paid reply card. Prospects wrote their name and phone number on the card, checked off a box noting their interest and popped it back in the mail. This was the "response" and the percentage of people who did that was the response "rate."

The concept of response rate still exists today, even though agreement about what constitutes "response" has gotten fuzzy for the modern marketing tools.

Take Twitter, for example. Is re-tweeting a "response"? How about clicking from tweet to webpage? Or is clicking from that webpage to a contact widget the "response"? Because the newer marketing tools are hazy on this point, let's stick with the older ones.

Email: Though lots of email involve links to websites, let's keep it simple and say the emails ask recipients to reply or call. A "response" happens when someone does that. The response rate for email is often less than one-quarter of one percent.

Mail: Letters or postcards go out and "response" is when someone contacts the sender. The response rate used to be about 1% to 3%. As email has become more annoying and mail more unusual, the response rate at the top of the range has increased to 5% or so.

Voicemail: You leave a message. When someone calls you back that's a response. Response rate for voicemail is about 3%.

Phone: You make a call. A response is when a human answers and is willing to hear you out. Response rate is between 25% and 33%.

Zowie! Personal touch, fast results, inexpensive, high response rate—these are excellent reasons to use telemarketing. Now let's clarify what you can and cannot accomplish as you use this marvelous marketing tool.

Myth #2: Gotta control the call

We can control some things when calling. But when we work hard to control things we cannot realistically control, we have poor results and get frustrated. When "control" includes attempting some light manipulation, a bit of self-loathing gets added on top.

The reality is we cannot make people do stuff. That is, we can't do that consistently without extreme effort (which is way too much work and hopefully not your style anyway). Here's what we can and cannot control using telemarketing:

- We can't make prospects answer the phone. Sure, we can often find better (or worse) days and times to reach people but the basic reality is that luck is involved.

- We cannot force people to give us their time or hear us out. There are no magic words to achieve that. However, we can prevent a high number of automatic no's, and we can keep the doors open.

- We cannot make people have a want or need for what we're offering. No value statement or script is so compelling it overrides our prospects' ability to choose. (If you doubt this particular reality, think about your own reaction when callers try this.) On the upside, we can often spark interest where there was none before, and we can keep the doors open.

Notice how keeping the doors open came up twice? That's because bad timing doesn't mean you're out of luck—unless you try too hard to push it.

To enjoy the greatest cold calling success with the least frustration, try to control only what you can actually control:

- Making the calls.

- Saying what you want to say

- Responding to what prospects say and do.

That's it. That's all you control. The good news is that's all you need to control to have terrific success with cold calling!

Myth #3: The compelling, unique value statement

The words we use to describe and think about cold calling impact how we feel, and what we try to accomplish. Again, we cannot compel—force—anyone to do anything. If we think we "should" be able to do that, we're just setting ourselves up for frustration.

As for unique, the bad news is the products or services you sell are probably not unique. (If they are, they're actually harder to sell.) Your company is probably not unique, either.

The good news is you do not have to sweat over the keyboard trying to invent some sort of unique message. You are your own unique value statement. Being yourself is part of what taps the power of the phone. Being yourself also helps draw the right prospects to you.

Myth #4: Apply in-depth research

There are a few sets of weird expectations related to myths about what research can do for cold calling.

The first myth to bust is the idea you should research prospects so you can offer them "solutions."

You cannot offer solutions without assuming there are problems to solve. Prospects don't like this assumptive message. They don't like any kind of assumption, but this one is particularly annoying because it says you know better than they do. There you are; a total stranger calling out of the blue, telling them they have problems but not to worry because you will save the day. See why that bugs people?

A related myth says you can use the research to show prospects you know their business or industry issues. In truth, using information mostly shows prospects you studied a few websites. And if those sites are not current, using that content is even less impressive.

The third research myth to bust is about using what you learned to personalize or customize each call to each prospect.

The idea is that personalizing will get more prospects' attention. It backfires because it's almost impossible to do this without also sounding assumptive. Customizing each call also puts way too much work into these prospects. You don't have enough information at this point to know if these prospects warrant that effort.

Doing too much research can also add a false sense of familiarity or rapport with prospects. When prospects don't reciprocate, it can feel like personal rejection and that's harder to bounce back from.

What's more, using information from websites and social media can creep prospects out. Logically, they know the information is out there—they often posted it—but many still feel slightly stalked when strangers use it.

Of course, you probably want to do some research, so what's the right amount? Research to get a general sense of what's going on, and for clues prospects *may* be interested in your services or products. That's it.

It's also worth noting that doing research is a traditional procrastination device. I myself used to walk many blocks to the local business library to spend hours researching companies located on the floors right above my office. The web just makes this procrastination much easier now.

Myth #5: Warming calls up

I already tackled this myth but it's so pervasive it's worth busting again. The things people do to try to warm calls up very rarely have a positive impact on results. Let me be crystal clear: there is usually zero difference in results.

It's just as important to know a significant percentage of people feel more nervous about making supposedly "warm" calls. The idea they're not supposed to feel that way only adds a whole layer of baggage.

Forget "warm" versus "cold." You feel the way you feel, and a call is a call is a call.

Myth #6: Making calls yourself looks bad

Lots of people worry prospects will think poorly of them because they placed a cold call. This concern is directly related to the idea only rookies and losers should have to make cold calls. I'll tackle that myth in a second, for now, here's the scoop:

The vast majority of prospects will think absolutely nothing about your making calls—it won't make an impression one way or the other.

Some prospects will be surprised and delighted to hear directly from the consultant, business owner, advisor, banker, broker, designer, etc.

Very few prospects will think poorly of your call. They fall into the same category of people who think you sound too young or too old, who don't like financial advisors because the stock market is gambling, who believe insurance brokers are all in cahoots, who don't want a website because they don't want the internet to spy on them... These prospects are NAP: Not a Prospect.

Myth #7: Only rookies and losers make cold calls

The root of this myth is actually that successful, experienced people do not make cold calls. Many of these folks even say things like, "I haven't made cold calls in years."

Experienced, successful people do indeed make cold calls. However, they don't necessarily refer to them as "cold," primarily because these calls don't resemble the kind of call they were taught to make. See the next page for what they are doing instead:

- They don't want to waste anyone's time (including their own) so they tend to get right to the point.

- They understand not every prospect is going to be a good fit, so they avoid an assumptive approach.

- They know prospects have to be open and ready to talk, so they don't push—which ensures they don't waste their own time, either.

- And they tend to feel comfortable with who they are as professionals, so they talk the way they normally talk.

In short, they make consultative style calls.

Summary: Train Your Brain

Part of what you need for success is a different model to use. That model is consultative style cold calling.

You also need to embrace some key concepts, which may involve changing some of your thinking. You are prospecting or marketing (not selling). Luck is a factor. There are lots of things you can do to put luck on your side and you'll learn about these throughout the book.

We cannot make people do things, so work on controlling only what you actually can control: making the calls, saying what you want to say, and responding to what prospects say and do. This is all you need to control to enjoy tremendous success.

Cold calling myths pile baggage onto calling and undermine your efforts at the same time. Knowing the truth helps set realistic expectations and an effective approach.

The most harmful myths are that you need to "warm" calls up, and that making calls means you are either a loser or a rookie. Both of these are baloney.

SCRIPTING BASICS

First Things First: Why Use Scripts?

Introduction to Natural Scripts

I have never let my schooling interfere with my education.

(Mark Twain)

Why Use Scripts?

SCRIPTS PLAY a big part in your cold calling success.

Your scripts guide you to use an effective consultative approach. Since you can write scripts in advance, you can also analyze and improve your approach in advance.

The action of drafting and refining scripts helps knowledge about consultative cold calling sink in, and then warms it up when needed. The impact is similar to how hitting balls at a driving range helps your game on the course.

A good script makes it easier to stay on track with less effort. Since you're not working as hard on what you want to say, you're more open to clues and cues from prospects. This frees you to have better give and take conversations when prospects want to do that. Scripts also strengthen your ability to respond to the unexpected, for the same reasons.

Good scripts keep you grounded by providing reminders of what's reasonable to achieve. This helps prevent frustration, as well as prevents many common errors.

Great scripts do all of that and sound just like you do when you're feeling relaxed and confident. The trouble is, we don't write like we talk.

A well-written version of that last sentence would be, "We don't speak the same way we write, which presents a challenge." Say that aloud and you can hear how stilted it sounds.

We run into similar problems when we try to write scripts that "sound" professional. For example, let's try to make the write/talk sentence more impressive. You might want to read the following aloud:

"We don't necessarily speak the same way we write, which generates significant issues for certain individuals as they seek to position themselves for success in dialogue with potential clients."

Can you even get that whole sentence out in one breath? Probably not. You have to force it out, which sounds awkward. Or you have to take a breath somewhere, which sounds like you're reading from a script.

All of the above is what makes calls sound canned, and feel uncomfortable.

Introduction to natural scripts

To sound and feel natural on the phone, you need to sound like you're talking, not reading. This means your guides—scripts—should not be written the same way you'd write most other things.

Of course, you probably spent a lot of time learning to write. You may even pride yourself on writing well; using good grammar, punctuating properly, and finding just the right word. Dropping these habits and building a new set of writing skills may take some effort and practice. The good news is there are just three things to keep in mind.

- When we talk, we breathe in-between sentences
- That means script sentences should be short
- And we should toss good grammar out the window

Grammar gets tossed because most of us don't talk that way. That's partly *because* we use shorter sentences. And partly because modern communication just doesn't involve proper grammar.

So go ahead and start sentences with "and." Feel free to end sentences with prepositions. Heck, feel free not to know what a preposition is.

People don't absorb longer sentences on the phone, anyway. In fact, most prospects will miss at least part of a grammatically correct complex sentence.

More good news

In order to learn new things, most of us need to see models to copy. We also need to see examples of common errors so we can avoid them. That's why this book includes so many before and after script examples. That's also why some of the other content purposely uses shorter sentences.

I'll also provide plenty of tips, starting with this one: To test your script sentences, pay attention to where you take a breath. If you have to take a breath somewhere within a sentence, it's probably too long.

More tips, later, including in the "Analyze the Other Guys" chapter.

CONTACT/PROSPECT CALLS

Script Formats & Why They Work

Busting the B2B Myth

Analyze the Other Guys

Examples of Effective Scripts

One day every major city in America will have a telephone.

(Alexander Graham Bell, slightly underestimating the impact of his invention)

Why "Contact/Prospect"?

YOUR CONTACT/PROSPECT SCRIPTS hold content you'll also use in other types of calls, including gatekeeper calls and voicemail messages. Before we get into these formats, I want to explain their title and help you avoid some common errors—including with your CRM.

Beware bossy CRM

Lots of callers and sales organizations want to define types of prospects. This process often generates too many categories with confusing titles, especially for prospects not yet in the sales pipeline. I recommend keeping things simple and realistic.

Sometimes we know the individuals we're calling are the "right" prospects. Sometimes we're not sure but we've got a name—a contact—and that's who we start with. This is where "contact/prospect" comes from.

You may want to title contacts/prospects differently than I have. For example, some people like to use "lead" in certain situations. I don't intend to try to boss you around about this but don't let your CRM boss you around, either. Make sure a CRM's definitions match yours, not the other way around. (More tips in the CRM Stuff section of the Savage and Greene blog.)

Definitely dump suspects and the decision maker

I am definitely going to be bossy about using "suspect" to define prospects, leads or whomever. Using verbal reminders not all prospects will become clients is a good idea but, jeez..."suspect"? Its definition is *to view with suspicion*. That negative perspective will come through to prospects and pull your own spirits down.

While I'm in mini-lecture mode, I want to note that searching for "the decision maker" when cold calling is a bad idea, too.

When you ask about the decision maker, the message to the listener is you assume it's not them. These individuals can often help you. Unfortunately, since you essentially told them you don't think they deserve much respect, they're not going to do that.

In addition, buying decisions often involve more than one person. If you look for the decider—as in single or main or most important—you can easily overlook or discount other important individuals.

Besides, the best time to find out about decision makers and decision process is when you're selling. Are you selling yet? Nope, not yet. Alright, lecture over. Time for the formats.

A note about how I show the parts of the script formats

Highlighting the parts of the script formats presented a bit of a quandary. Using all-uppercase, all of the time, could be really irritating. The other option is to capitalize the first letters, e.g. Who You Are. But some parts—like that one—are also everyday phrases for which capitalizing would look odd.

Eventually, I decided to use both. I use all-uppercase when introducing formats, and when showing each part next to an example of what's said. I capitalize the first letters when I want to highlight parts of a script format but do not want to use uppercase.

Neither of those are used when I show what not to do and explain why. As for everyday phrases... I'm pretty sure readers will understand that sometimes saying who you are should not be shown as "saying Who You Are."

Contact/Prospect Script Formats

There are three Contact/Prospect formats. All three are shown here; however, the format used to qualify with questions in covered in the qualifying section.

Format A

Who you are
Why you're calling
Ask for next step
Schedule
Prep, if desired

Format B

Who you are
Why you're calling
Ask permission
Give information (and transition)
Ask for next step
Schedule
Prep, if desired

Format B with Qualifying Questions (see the qualifying section)

Who you are
Why you're calling
Ask permission
Give information (and transition)
Ask qualifying questions
Respond to answers
Ask for next step
Schedule
Prep, if desired

Introducing Format A

THE FULL FORMAT is Who You Are, Why You're Calling, Ask For the Next Step, Schedule, and Prep (if desired). Let's put Schedule and Prep aside for now and go over the first three parts.

Who You Are

This is the first part of all script formats. *Duh*, I know, but there are some nuances to saying who you are. I'll cover them later.

Why You're Calling

The core reason for most of these calls is you'd like the opportunity to explore the fit—you'd like to have a sales conversation. In this format, you put that right out there, front and center.

Ask for Next Step

And then you ask for that sales conversation.

Example script

As you can see by the example below, scripts using this format are short and to the point:

WHO YOU ARE: My name is Shawn, and I'm with a sales training company.

WHY YOU'RE CALLING: I'd like to see if our training programs would provide excellent value for your business.

ASK FOR THE NEXT STEP: Can we set up a meeting to explore that?

Why Format A works well

In this format, there's no lengthy introduction of yourself or your company, little to no mention of problems your services solve, no benefit statements, and no talk about letters you sent. Instead, you simply say you'd like to have a sales conversation and then ask prospects if they're willing to do that.

This format works very well on the prospects' end of the line because they're already aware of the reason for your call. By saying it so clearly and directly, you show respect for their intelligence and their time.

The key to this format's power is to use consultative wording such as, *see if, may have* and *explore*. Consultative wording shows prospects you're not assuming your products or services would benefit them. This demonstrates respect for each prospect's unique wants, needs and interests—because you're not acting as if you know what those are.

Consultative wording helps you, too, by keeping your feet on the ground. The reality is your products and services are not a good fit for everyone, nor is every prospect a good fit for you.

It's important to note the format ends with an Ask: you ask for a sales conversation. By asking clearly, you get a clear answer and that means you know if you're moving into selling or continuing to market with each prospect.

Pros and cons of Format A

Many prospects like Format A's short and sweet approach. That said, it tends to appeal most strongly to prospects who happen to be looking for your products or services when you call.

On the downside, you don't have opportunity to share information that may spark interest.

Callers who use this format tend to project an easy confidence. On the other hand, using this format may take more guts.

TIP: Write your own Format A first

When you start working on your own scripts, work on Format A first. Work on Format A first even if you don't think you'll use it or are not sure it will work in your market—and no matter how challenging drafting it may be.

Learning how to say why you're calling in direct and consultative ways is the biggest hurdle for most people. Format A focuses on this part, so working on it first shortens your learning curve overall.

Introducing Format B

THIS FORMAT IS longer, so here it is again for easy reference:

- Who You Are
- Why You're Calling
- Ask Permission
- Give Information (and Transition)
- Ask For Next Step
- Schedule
- Prep, If Desired

The powerhouse: Give Information

This time we'll start in the middle—with Give Information—because that is the format's powerhouse.

There's a huge variety of things you can do within this part of your script. You can talk about products and services, and how your clients use them. You can cover your approach or philosophy. You can give one or two examples of problems solved, or touch on current topics and relate them to your services.

That's just a handful of what you can do within Give Information. Notice you are giving information <u>to</u> prospects, rather than trying to get information <u>from</u> them. This is powerful because you can differentiate yourself in meaningful ways, as well as prevent common objections.

Giving information is also powerful because it sometimes prompts interest where there was none, and it helps develop relationships because it lets your perspective and personality come through.

You can use Give Information to prevent a lot of push back because you're not annoying prospects with nosy questions. On the other hand, you can also use Give Information to pave the way for qualifying questions—or to qualify without asking questions at all.

All of that may look like a lot to accomplish in a cold call. These calls are indeed longer than Format A. To explain why the entire Format B works well, let's loop back to the top of the format.

Who You Are

I'll cover the nuances later but here's one tip right now: say who you are before you ask for the prospect. If the first thing you say is to ask, "Is this Joyce?" you are invading their space, which often generates a little push-back.

Why You're Calling

In Format B, Why has to cover two things:

- The core reason for your call (you'd like to have a sales conversation).

- And how you would like to use their time right now, in this moment, and in this phone call.

You can handle those things in either order. However, both have to be covered to avoid annoying prospects with an unstated agenda.

Ask Permission

Now that you've told prospects how you'd like to use their time, ask if it's okay to continue the call. As long as you continue only when you have permission, this demonstrates respect for their time.

Asking permission works far better than trying various sneaky techniques to prevent a "no." In fact, people are more inclined to give you permission when you simply ask for it.

Asking permission also uses your time well. When people are not interested or do not have time, it's better you know now than thirty seconds from now.

Give Information (and Transition)

As I explained, proactively giving information has a lot of power and there are tons of options for this part. At the end of giving information is a "transition" statement. This statement signals that what you're saying is about to change direction.

Without a transition statement, you go from giving information to asking for a next step. In your head this makes total sense but it takes prospects by surprise a little bit. That tiny surprise can generate a tiny bit of push back. The sudden switch also adds a canned, awkward effect. Transition statements prevent all of these problems.

Transition statements are important but easy to miss, so they're marked in the examples.

Ask For The Next Step

This format also ends with a clear Ask. Asking for the next step is not about whether they think what you've described would have value (because that's jumping ahead into selling). You're not going to ask if you can email them something (because that's not the real reason for the call). You're going to ask to have a sales conversation—because that's what you would like to see happen.

Script example

WHO YOU ARE: This is Steve. I'm calling from Computer Crossing.

WHY YOU'RE CALLING: We'd like to see if our tech support services would be a good fit for you. I'd like to tell you a little bit about what we do. And then see where things may go from there.

ASK PERMISSION: Do you have a couple minutes?

GIVE INFORMATION: We can handle almost any kind of technical issue for PCs, tablets and Macs. Transferring data from old computers to new. Setting up networks and getting new hires ready. Software training, troubleshooting, going mobile. Helping clients figure out if they should buy new or fix old. Things like that.

Our focus is companies with less than 50 computer and device users. That includes people working solo, and home office support. Clients say they like having us take the techie stuff off their hands, and our free loaner laptops. We also get a lot of compliments about our pricing because it's so flexible. That's the overview (Transition statement).

ASK FOR NEXT STEP: Whether you've got in-house tech talent or not, I'd like the chance to see if our services would be a good fit. Can we set up a meeting?

Some points about the above example

To avoid an unstated agenda and leverage this format's full power, Why You're Calling has to cover two things. Let me parse them out of the example for you:

"We'd like to see if our tech support services would be a good fit for you." This is the core reason for the call.

"I'd like to tell you a little bit about what we do." This is what Steve wants to do right now, in this phone call.

"And then see where things may go from there." This wraps back to the core reason, so the WHY sounds cohesive.

Notice that Ask Permission is concise, direct, and simple.

As for Give Information, you might look at that example and think it needs some changes. Maybe you'd focus on just one aspect of tech support. Maybe you'd say, "We work with solo entrepreneurs up to companies with 50 employees." Or maybe you'd script that and then discover it's too hard to enunciate "entrepreneurs." Maybe you'd focus on examples of how the pricing is flexible because you think that feature is most important. Maybe you think the wording is too informal or not descriptive enough.

All of the above are valid, effective ways to go. Choose based on what's important to you, and let your scripts reflect who you are. By expressing that in your calls, you leverage your secret weapon: your personality.

Pros and cons for Format B

This format's strengths center on what you can do with Give Information. This includes differentiating yourself, preventing or defusing objections, and qualifying without asking direct questions.

However, it takes some practice to come up with good Give Information content that also sounds natural. This book will help you get there.

Format B works well with those prospects who say, "You've got two minutes." This format also helps develop good relationships from the start, even when prospects are not ready to move on to sales conversations.

A common downside for the caller (you) is Format B can feel like it takes too long. The majority of these calls take 90 seconds or less—many people have timed them—but it can still feel strange at first.

It's also important to know most prospects don't consider these calls overly long. You have permission to use a bit of their time, remember?

Challenges with scripting Format B: Mismatch and getting stuck

To explain these challenges, I need to go back to one of the things that drive people crazy about receiving cold calls—something you want to avoid.

One of the main irritants is when the caller says they're calling about X but the call is really about Y. For example, they say they're doing a survey on vacation habits but it becomes clear they're really selling timeshare rentals. These callers have a mismatch on purpose, to sneak up on the real reason.

When writing a Format B script, some callers have a mismatch by accident. They don't realize the stated reason for why they're calling doesn't match the rest of their script. Here's how this happens:

When we're writing something that's challenging (e.g., something that uses a new calling approach) we tend to work on each part one by one.

After we're done writing, we tend to review each part one by one, from the top on down. Did I say both parts of why I'm calling? Check. Do the words sound like me? Check. Did I use consultative wording? Check. Did I clearly ask for a sales conversation? Check.

Because we're looking at Why and Give Information separately, even a major mismatch can slip right by us. But that mismatch will stand out and make a negative impression on listeners. The mismatch makes us sound less professional, less sure of ourselves, and even less trustworthy.

Another problem that comes up when writing Format B is getting stuck. We come up with a good way to say why we're calling, cruise through asking permission and then...stall out.

Sometimes that happens because at some level we recognize what we're writing for Give Information doesn't quite match what we wrote for Why We're Calling. Our brain sends up a red flag and slows thinking down.

Sometimes people get stuck because their idea for Give Information sounded good as they started their script but doesn't hold up when they try to expand on it. They feel committed to the idea and try to slog through.

Both problems (mismatch and getting stuck) can be avoided or fixed using the same writer's trick: write the introduction last. Or, in this case, write Give Information first and then work on Why You're Calling, as described in the tip below.

TIP: Start in the middle

Use a writers' trick and write the introduction last. In this case: write Give Information first and then look at what you have.

Is it an introduction? An overview? One or two examples? A snapshot? A little bit about your services, what you do, or how you approach your work with customers?

Once you've identified what you're doing with Give Information, go back to the top of your script. Use that brief description in Why You're Calling so the two match.

Both Formats: Schedule & Prep, if Desired

ALL CONTACT/PROSPECT FORMATS include these three parts at the end:

- Ask For Next Step

- Schedule

- Prep, if Desired

After you ask for the next step—a sales conversation—prospects will answer with a yes or no. I'll deal with "no" in later chapters. When the answer is yes, you want to schedule that sales conversation.

Schedule a separate sales conversation

A while back, I introduced the importance and value of drawing a mental line between prospecting (telemarketing) and selling. Drawing a line between the two activities is equally valuable. Instead of moving right into a sales conversation, schedule it for later. Here's why:

- Remember you have interrupted prospects. They probably don't have time right now to drop what they are doing and put their full attention to a sales conversation.

- You'll probably have a more successful sales conversation if you prepare for it. Scheduling for a later time or date gives you freedom to do that.

- Scheduling sales conversations for later also helps you focus on prospecting. You want to let yourself get into the swing of cold calling by making a bunch of calls in a row.

As a best practice: set a later date and time for the sales conversation (later the same day is fine). Be sure you also determine if it will occur on the phone or in person. If it's to be in person, where, and so on.

"Schedule" is in the formats mostly as a reminder of the above. It is the only part in these formats you do not necessarily need to script out. However, some callers find scripting it out is helpful, as shown in the Format A example below.

When now is best

Of course, if the prospect wants to have that sales conversation now, you might want to go for it. Prepare a separate guide for sales conversations and have it ready for use—do not blend this into your cold calling scripts.

Prep, if desired

"Prep" stands for "prepare for the sales conversation." It's optional because leaving it out won't hurt calling or selling results.

Prep involves asking just a few questions to help yourself get ready for the sales conversation.

It's very important to keep yourself from jumping into selling when you ask Prep questions. These should <u>not</u> be questions about wants or needs, who their current provider is, how they make decisions, etc.. Hold questions like those for the sales conversation.

Prep questions are about things such as: any issues the prospect wants to be sure are covered; any materials or data they may want to see; who else will attend the meeting; and how much time they can give you. (That's just a few examples.)

If you use Prep, you should write it into your script. I'll give you more guidelines in the next section. For now, here's a full example of Schedule and Prep in Format A, followed by a couple tips for using what Prep uncovered.

Example Format A

WHO YOU ARE: My name is Sara Jones. I'm a commercial banker with Community Bank.

WHY YOU'RE CALLING: We'd like the opportunity to compete for your business. I'd like to start with an introductory meeting and then go from there.

ASK FOR NEXT STEP: Are you open to doing that?

SCHEDULE: May I come to you, and get a tour of the business? What date and time would work for you?

PREP: I've got a few questions so I can prepare to use our time well.

If others will attend our meeting, may I have their names?

Are there any hot topics or issues I should be ready to cover?

Aside from the tour, about how much time will you be able to give me?

Using the answers to your Prep questions

The above example includes a preface that explains why Sara (the caller) is asking questions. Including a preface like that is a best practice, and you'll see more examples in later chapters.

As the prospect answers your questions, note them down. However, do not respond back unless it's clearly pressing or they ask you to do that. Instead: acknowledge what they said, say you look forward to seeing them or talking with them at the date and time you've set. Hang up and move on to the next dial.

Go back to your notes as you prepare to meet with the prospect—that's what Prep is for.

Summary, and Next

Start working on your Contact/Prospect scripts first because the content will be used in the rest of your scripts, including gatekeeper and voicemail scripts. The part that carries over most directly is this one: Why You're Calling.

Format A focuses on saying Why You're Calling, along with a nice clear Ask For the Next Step. If you work on this format first, the rest of the scripts will come more easily.

Format A and Format B have their pros and cons. Some callers use both formats, some have a preference for one. As long as you apply a consultative approach they both work very well.

Speaking of applying a consultative approach... There's nothing like ripping apart bad scripts to show you how to succeed with good ones.

Analyze the Other Guys

THERE ARE FIVE examples; each show the most common mistakes and problems. Some bad example scripts came from one individual, some blend errors from two or three.

I've changed the names, of course. I've also changed some of the industries. Even though each bad example identifies the kind of industry or caller, that's just for context. Bankers, consultants, insurance brokers, web designers, janitorial services, financial advisors—the mistakes tend to be the same.

Most of the examples are B2B, which brings us to yet another myth that needs busting.

Myth: B2B and B2C calls differ

The idea here is that when we call business owners and executives we need to use a more sophisticated approach. We also need to get right to the point because these guys are busy and their time is valuable.

Okay, let's accept all of that as true. What on earth happens to these people when they leave work and go home? Are they suddenly less sophisticated? Less deserving of respect? Less busy?

That's why this myth is my favorite—it's just plain silly. Calls to businesses and calls to consumers are the same.

Before and after script examples

It may help to know how the next section is laid out.

First I show an example of what not to do. The bad example shows the entire unfortunate script. These are not shown with quotation-marks or italics, you'll just see a "Bad Example" heading and then the original in all its ineffective glory (and in a different font).

These are real scripts! I've got tons of these from people who submitted them before attending training, and from calls I get in my office or at home. If any seem familiar, it's because you, too, have received or made calls just like them.

Next I'll rip each bad script apart, bit by bit. Sorry, that wasn't very nice, was it? I meant to say I'll use applicable portions to illustrate errors, problems and so on.

Finally, I'll show you revised scripts in Format A and Format B that prevent problems and errors, along with tips and pointers. Scripts are shown on one page, as often as possible.

Please note none of these scripts include qualifying—that's covered in a separate section.

Bad Example #1
Commercial Insurance Broker

This is Mary Hotsenpiller with Risk Management Consultants, which provides insurance solutions.

The reason for my call is to talk with you about our extensive experience in guiding clients to risk management solutions because most organizations lack effective expertise in this area.

Which would be more convenient for you, this ___ or ___ ?

What not to do, and why

"This is Mary Hotsenpiller with Risk Management Consultants, which provides insurance solutions."

Let us commence the ripping apart with Mary's last name. The name 'Hotsenpiller' is probably unfamiliar to many prospects and this can be a problem.

When prospects hear a name they don't quite get, there's a teeny blip of "what?" in their mind. That blip is not one of interest—it's a blip of annoyance.

Similar annoyance can occur when the first name is unusual. Men named Lynn, Lesley and Jocelyn run into this, just like women named Michael and Shawn do.

Of course, familiarity varies. Last names like Boudin, Nguyen, and Ljunggren are common in some places and not so common in others. Ditto for first names like Asher, Rolf and Maricela.

Also notice Mary made her last name "Hotsenpiller with Risk Management Consultants." To avoid that she needs a comma to help her pause. Or she could say her name and then say, "I'm with Risk Management Consultants."

The sentence is also a bit too long, so Mary may sound canned as she forces it all out in one breath.

On the positive side of things, Mary explained what her company does. This is important because the company name doesn't do that by itself, nor is the company well-known. By adding the explanation she provides a bit of context for the call.

Those are some of the pitfalls that can occur as we open our call. Let's take a look at how to avoid them.

TIPS: How to say Who You Are

Let's start with your own name:

- If your entire name is hard for people to grasp, say your first name only.

  I ran into this when I first started calling. Instead of "Shawn Greene," people heard "Maureen." That didn't happen when I just used "Shawn."

- If your last name is hard for people to get, say your first name only.

- If people don't easily hear your first name, slow down so you enunciate more clearly.

Remember the idea is to avoid giving prospects a tweak of annoyance because they don't quite get what you said. However, it is not important prospects hear your name correctly. It's okay if prospects think Ms. Michael Dillon's first name is "Michelle." She can correct that later.

Now let's cover using a company name:

- Does the company name provide context for the call—does the name say what the company does? If your company name says what it does, such as "Oak River Bank" and "ABC Home Repair," then use it.

- Is the company name well known? If so, this often provides context all by itself. For example, most prospects know or have heard of "Oracle."

- If you are calling from a well-known company but a lesser-known department, you may want to add a short explanation, like so: "I'm calling from the analytics group of Oracle."

If your company name does not say what it does and is not well known, you have a couple options:

- One option is to add a very brief explanation, like Mary did.

- The other option is not to use the company name at all. For example:

  "I'm with a company that provides risk management advice" or *"I'm a risk management consultant"* or *"I'm a commercial lines broker."*

Sometimes company names are easily confused. For example, ADP and ADT sound alike but offer very different services. In this situation:

- You can enunciate the company name more slowly. Unfortunately, this may sound and feel awkward, so test-drive it to see if that's the case.

- If speaking slowly doesn't work for you, add a little explanation or leave the company name out and use just the explanation.

Back to what not to do, and why

"The reason for my call is to talk with you about our extensive experience in guiding clients to risk management solutions because most organizations lack effective expertise in this area."

This single sentence in the script illustrates six common problems.

Problem #1: Mary doesn't say she'd like to explore the business fit, she just says she wants to chat. The unstated agenda undermines her credibility at the same time it irritates most prospects.

Problem #2: Mary uses the phrase, "The reason..."

We hear this phrase in two situations. We hear it when we're getting bad news ("The reason I've called you into my office is that we have to let you go"). And we hear it in cold calls, which means you can't help but sound canned if you use it.

Problem #3: Um... Mary pretty much insults the prospect because she says the organization lacks expertise. Even prospects who would like some help will find this statement annoying because it's coming from a stranger.

Problem #4: Try the sentence aloud and you'll find it is too long. Mary will have to force her breath to get it all out, or will take a breath in a strange spot. Either way, it's going to sound canned.

Semi-problem #5: Using the word "solutions" may sound tired and empty, but this depends on what's going on in her marketplace.

Ten years ago Mary probably would have said, "meet risk management <u>needs</u>," which eventually became overused. At this point, using "solutions" instead of "needs" may or may not be overused, too.

Problem #6: Mary may have failed to let her personality shine through, but it's hard to tell just by looking at the script. Perhaps Mary is as condescending and boring as she sounds here, or maybe she's using a bad script.

"Which would be more convenient for you, this (date/time) or (date/time)?"

Ah, the good ol' Tuesday at 10 or Thursday at 3. Throwing the word "convenient" in there cannot erase the trite assumption of this question and so it will mostly backfire.

This question doesn't help draw that important line between prospecting and selling, either, because Mary did not ask the prospect for a sales conversation. And because Mary didn't ask for that, any meeting will be on shakier footing than it needs to be.

Enough with the ripping apart, let's fix Mary's script!

Introduction to Mary's revised scripts

To help the script format sink in, you'll see each element along with the script text.

As you read the examples, remember some parts are used only when applicable. For example, Schedule and Prep are only used when prospects have agreed to have a sales conversation.

You may want to pay extra attention to punctuation and sentence structure. Sentences are purposely short because that's the way we talk. (You may want to say the scripts aloud to get used to writing that way.)

Please note Mary is calling a list which shows when prospects' insurance expires/renews (the "X date"). She is calling earlier than usual on purpose and wants to prevent objections about this.

These examples use phrases that are familiar to Mary's prospects, they understand what a commercial lines broker does, and what "risk management" means. The examples also include the word "solutions" because our pretend broker likes it.

Revised Script: Format A

WHO YOU ARE: My name is Mary. I'm a commercial lines broker with Risk Management Consultants.

WHY YOU'RE CALLING: We'd like the opportunity to earn your business. I'm aware your key lines renewal period is about three months away. I'd like to meet with you soon to see if our extensive expertise would provide valuable guidance at that time.

ASK FOR NEXT STEP: Are you open to meeting to evaluate our services?

SCHEDULE: I'd like about one hour of your time. What date and time work for you?

PREP: So I can prepare to use our time well, I have a few questions.

- Are there any particular issues I should be ready to cover?

- We have programs designed for your industry. Shall I bring program materials to leave with you?

- Will any others attend this meeting?

Thank you for that information. I look forward to seeing you. I also understand schedules can change. I'll call to confirm and if something comes up, let me know and we'll reschedule.

Notes about the above example Format A

Insurance brokers like Mary often prefer to work with clients based on service and expertise, not insurance rate. It's harder to sell this kind of relationship when the renewal is right around the corner. At the same time, one of the most common objections is that the renewal is far away.

In her script, Mary defuses the timing issue by making this statement, *"I'm aware your key lines renewal period is about three months away."* She doesn't add 'but' or anything like that, she simply acknowledges the timeframe.

Mary goes on to say, *"I'd like to meet with you* soon *to see if our extensive expertise would provide valuable guidance* at that time." This statement connects the present to the renewal time, which helps prevent objections about it being too early.

That statement also positions the kind of relationship Mary prefers to have with clients. Using it helps draw those prospects to her.

Those preferences and common objections are not unique to insurance brokers. If they strike a bell for you, a similar approach can work for you, too.

Notice Mary's script asks for a one hour meeting. This is the amount of time she genuinely would like to have for a first sales conversation.

That is a best practice. Forget the over-used 15 or 20 minutes—ask for the amount you actually want. What's the worst that can happen? If they say that's too long you can adjust.

Mary's script includes three Prep questions. Again, these questions are designed to help prepare for a sales conversation.

Right after the questions her script shows, *"Thank you for that information."* This scripting acknowledges the prospect's answers at the same time it helps prevent Mary from responding to the answers and jumping into selling.

Her script wraps things up with two more best practices: she'll confirm, and she'll reschedule if needed.

Revised Format B on the next page...

Revised Script: Format B

WHO YOU ARE: My name is Mary. I'm a commercial lines broker with Risk Management Consultants.

WHY YOU'RE CALLING: I'm aware your key lines renewal period is about three months away. I'd like to briefly introduce my expertise. And then see if you're open to giving us the opportunity to earn your business.

ASK PERMISSION: Is this a good time?

GIVE INFORMATION: Thank you. You may be aware there are a limited number of carriers with good programs for restaurants. We believe this highlights the importance of a broker's ability to act as consultant. We further believe consultants must have deep knowledge of clients' challenges to do that.

In order to provide expertise along with insurance solutions, our brokers focus on certain industries. Restaurants is one of mine. My restaurant experience began in my parents' café. Familiarity with challenges literally began at the kitchen table. Continued as I worked my way through college at large restaurants. Solidified over the past many years as a broker.

I blend this broad industry experience with knowing each client as a unique entity. Because each has its risk management strengths and challenges. That is just an overview (Transition).

I'd like to explore the possibility our firm's extensive risk management expertise would provide value.

ASK FOR NEXT STEP: Are you open to meeting soon to evaluate our services?

SCHEDULE: I'd like about one hour of your time. What date and time work for you?

Notes about the above example Format B

When you say why you're calling using this format, you need to cover two things.

One thing is what you'd like to do right now, in this phone call. Mary's script covers this with *"briefly introduce my expertise."*

The other thing to cover is the core reason—you'd like to have a sales conversation. This example uses *"And then see if you're open to giving us the opportunity to earn your business."*

Notice how that sentence starts with *"and then."* That is not proper grammar, it is good script writing.

This example uses *"Is this a good time?"* for asking permission. Some worry this question gives prospects an easy out. Well, if prospects don't want to give you some time, no fancy phrasing will change that. However, there are lots of ways to ask permission. If you don't like that one, there are many others to use.

Notice Give Information begins with *"Thank you."* This is a nice touch but it's only included in Mary's script because she wants to remember to say it. In other words, it wouldn't come naturally for her (see the tip below).

The content of Give Information aligns with how Mary described it when she said Why she's calling. If it didn't match up, the call would project an unprofessional image.

TIP: If Mary had drafted her script and then realized the Why and Give Information didn't match, she should re-draft the Why. This is almost always easier than the other way around.

You might have noticed this Give Information example uses somewhat personal content. Some commercial insurance brokers find this is an effective way to differentiate themselves, some find it's best to cover more technical content. There's no right or wrong here.

Near the end of Give Information the script says, *"That is just an overview (Transition)."* This transition statement signals a change to prospects, which helps prevent push-back.

After the transition statement the script shows: *"I'd like to explore the possibility our firm's extensive risk management expertise would provide value. Are you open to meeting soon to evaluate our services?"*

The second sentence is the Ask (underlined just to highlight it for you). Note the wording is a direct and clear request for a sales conversation.

Last but not least, there is no Prep in this example. Including Prep is optional. Some people feel their Format B scripts are on the long side and including Prep would make them too long.

If you feel your scripts are already long but you want to include Prep, ask permission to ask Prep questions. (You'll see an example of this later.)

TIP: "Great!" and other comments

I often see scripts which include things like "Good morning," "Good afternoon," and "Great!" People tend to include these in an effort to make their scripts sound and feel more natural. Unfortunately, including them usually makes scripts sound and feel *less* natural. Here are guidelines to help you avoid that.

If you normally and automatically say things like "good morning," do not include them in your script because doing so will make the words sound overly-scripted. The same goes for things like, "Great!" I'm not telling you not to say those things! Just leave them out of the written script and say them as you normally would.

On the other hand; if saying things like that is something you want to add to your communication style, DO put them in your script. The same goes for "good afternoon" and "thank you." Alas, adding "Great!" doesn't help us sound enthusiastic. If you don't normally use it, do not add it.

One more tip: remove those little comments from your scripts once they come naturally.

TIP: How to dump "needs" and "solutions"

Certain words and phrases sound canned because they are over-used, or meaningless to us as callers.

Over-use is a matter of timing. The first callers to talk about "needs" probably made a great impression. At the time this book was written, the word has been trite for years but it could get hot again.

As for being meaningful or not, this depends on the caller, not the prospect. Callers who truly believe they offer solutions to significant problems don't sound canned when they say "solutions." Callers who use the word because that's what everybody else says sound scripted.

If you've been using "needs" or "solutions" and want to drop them, it may just be a matter of literally dropping them. For example:

"Your banking needs" becomes "your banking" or "your bank."

"Expertise along with insurance solutions" becomes "expertise along with insurance."

"Manufacturing equipment solutions designed to improve your bottom line" becomes "manufacturing equipment designed to improve your bottom line."

If simply dropping the words doesn't quite work, reword the whole sentence or entire description. This often requires us to reconsider what we're selling and how we want to describe it. That can be an excellent exercise because it generates more powerful scripts and better calling results.

Bad Example #2
Marketing Consultant

Good morning/afternoon Mr/Mrs ___. My name is Richard Sanderburg. I am a Consultant with ABC Marketing.

How are you?

I'm just calling to introduce myself. (pause)

Mr/Mrs ___ what kind of marketing does your organization ___ currently utilize? (response)

How is business as a result? I hope everything is going well. (analyze for sales opportunities)

Well, Mr/Mrs ____, I'm glad/sorry to hear about that. We here at ABC Marketing specialize in meeting the needs of organizations just like yours and I'm certain we will do the same for you, too. We partner with our clients from strategy to results.

By the way, are you the person who makes decisions about marketing?

What not to do, and why

"Good morning/afternoon Mr/Mrs ___."

Including things like "good morning" in your script can end up making your calls sound canned. Richard has a different/added problem: the slash mark.

The idea behind using a slash mark is to make it easier to remember good morning versus good afternoon but the slash mark actually makes using the script harder. Your brain has to read the whole thing—morning slash afternoon—and choose the correct one. Same goes for choosing Mr. or Mrs. or Ms.

Sure, choosing happens in a split second, but it still adds more work for your brain. In addition, many people stop seeing or processing the slash mark and accidentally say "Good morning afternoon." Oops.

Be careful about using Mr. or Mrs., too. As someone named Shawn Greene, I've received approximately 6 billion calls for Mr. Greene, and have often been addressed as Mrs. Greene (I'm not married to someone whose last name is Greene). I'm pretty patient with calls like that but your prospects may not be.

Using Mr., Mrs., or Ms. at all is one of those judgment calls. Start with your own preference for being addressed, then consider whether using these is formal enough for you or too formal. Consider your prospects' preferences last because prospects vary. A lot. If you're unsure, test drive your own preference and adjust as needed.

"My name is Richard Sanderburg. I am a Consultant with ABC Marketing."

Great job on not making his last name smoosh in with the rest. Richard Sanderburg has a nice ring to it and most prospects will probably hear the name clearly. Alas, Richard capitalized "consultant" and that may prompt him to say the word with an odd inflection.

"How are you?"

Uh oh, there it is, the thing that annoys people most about getting cold calls.

"I'm just calling to introduce myself. (pause)"

Problem # 1 with the above is the word "just."

In cold calling land "just" means "only," as in he is <u>only</u> calling to introduce himself. That would be fine if Richard planned to introduce himself and then close the call but that's not what he plans to do. He has other reasons for the call and prospects know that. The unstated agenda undermines Richard's credibility and generates push-back.

Problem #2 is Richard does not "introduce" himself much at all. In fact, he barely introduces the company and doesn't really say anything about himself!

The mismatch between what Richard <u>says</u> he's going to do and what he <u>actually</u> does also undermines his credibility, as well as projects an unprofessional image.

See the "(pause)" in that part of the script? That's problem #3. He plans to pause after stating he's calling to introduce himself.

Richard hopes prospects will fill that pause by saying something. In other words, he hopes to manipulate his prospects into responding. It's benign manipulation—he's not trying to rip them off or anything—but it's still manipulative and it's still going to be annoying.

Why manipulation backfires

Manipulative techniques like pausing or asking questions that are supposedly hard to say "no" to backfire for several reasons.

The majority of prospects know you're trying to manipulate them and find it annoying (as would you). The attempt prompts many prospects to refuse to continue with the call. Some of them get nasty and that's no fun to deal with, either.

Even more problems occur with polite prospects. They fill that pause with a response, gritting their teeth at the same time. These prospects let the call continue but resist the whole way in a genteel manner. As soon as they're able to close the call, they do. They have to think about it, have a meeting to run to, etc.

Since most people are on the polite end of the spectrum, the caller ends up slogging through a lot of calls. He doesn't hear "no" but he doesn't hear "yes," either.

Back to what not to do, and why

"Mr/Mrs ___ what kind of marketing does your organization ___ currently utilize? (response)

How is business as a result? I hope everything is going well. (analyze for sales opportunities)"

Asking questions is invasive and tends to annoy prospects. This is true even for business-oriented questions like the above. Some prospects will cut off the call as quickly as possible because they're so irritated. Others (those polite people) will answer the questions and become increasingly annoyed at the same time.

It's also important to note that when prospects answer questions in cold calls, the quality of the information is relatively poor. You've interrupted them, their mind is mostly on other things, you're invading their space... They're not going to share information at a meaningful level at this point.

One of the biggest issues for Richard is actually the part where he plans to analyze prospects' responses to his last question. In his script, he is telling himself to analyze for "sales opportunities."

Richard is not yet in a sales situation. By jumping ahead in his mind, he is less focused on what's happening with each prospecting call. His expectations are also out of whack with what's reasonable, which may create a lot of frustration. All of this is unproductive and all of this is reinforced by the note he included in his script.

"Well, Mr/Mrs ____, I'm glad/sorry to hear about that. We here at ABC Marketing specialize in meeting the needs of organizations just like yours and I'm certain we will do the same for you, too. We partner with our clients from strategy to results."

This particular bad example was provided by one person, who laughed when I asked how often he accidentally said "glad sorry" instead of one or the other. As I expected, he'd done that quite a few times, even after he added space so his script showed "glad / sorry."

But let's put the counterproductive punctuation aside. Take another look at this part of the script. Think about the implications of a script which comments on prospects' answers before Richard actually hears them.

Here is what that means: the prospects' answers are almost meaningless. And if the prospects' answers are almost meaningless, why ask the questions?

As Richard would tell you, the hope is that asking questions gets prospects to talk, gives him a chance to highlight value specific to their needs, and qualify them. That's the hope. In reality, these things rarely occur.

What's more, scripting responses to prospects' answers sets up a Catch-22. On the one hand, their answers are still varied enough so that a prepared response can only be generic. That's why Richard's script says his firm meets the needs of companies just like the prospect's, no matter what the prospect actually says.

On the other hand, most prospects will not be impressed by a generic response. They went through all that trouble to answer his nosy questions and didn't get information in return—information he said he was going to provide as he started the call.

This part of Richard's script also assumes his company can meet <u>all</u> prospects' wants and needs. Most prospects reject that kind of assumption and it can get Richard into hot water, too. What if he has a sales conversation with the prospect and realizes he does not want their business?

The second sentence in this part of his script is too long (try it aloud). Richard will have to force it out or pause in a weird place.

And then, right after he states his elevator-speechy tag line, Richard makes the final mistake in his script: "By the way, are you the person who makes decisions about marketing?"

By the way, Richard says, are you the person I really want to talk to? This transparent attempt to qualify the person on the phone will make Richard look self-centered.

Introduction to Richard's revised scripts

Richard's original script has two hints of content we can use: marketing strategy, and business resulting from the strategy. The revised scripts expand on these hints.

Again; it can be helpful to pay close attention to punctuation and sentence length. Reading the examples aloud can also help you get used to writing scripts.

Please note that I'll use "(T)" to identify transitions from this point, on. I'll also use "Give Info" instead of "Give Information."

There are four Format A scripts. There are one and one-half Format B scripts.

Revised Script: Format A

WHO YOU ARE: My name is Richard Sanderburg. I'm a consultant with ABC Marketing.

WHY YOU'RE CALLING: We work with businesses on their marketing strategy, implementation and maintenance. And we often emphasize maintenance because results are so important. I'd like to see if our services would be a good fit for your organization.

ASK FOR NEXT STEP: I'd like to set up a phone meeting and show you some project samples to start. Can we do that?

Another Format A

WHO YOU ARE: My name is Richard Sanderburg. I'm a consultant with ABC Marketing.

WHY YOU'RE CALLING: We do many kinds of marketing. Including social media, website design and web based marketing. I'd like to see if our services would be a good fit.

ASK FOR NEXT STEP: I'd like to set up a phone meeting to start. Show you some samples. Learn about what you're doing. See where things may go from there. Can we do that?

One more Format A

WHO YOU ARE: My name is Richard Sanderburg. I'm a consultant with ABC Marketing.

WHY YOU'RE CALLING: We do many kinds of marketing. Including social media and web based marketing. We work with mid-size businesses. And emphasize helping clients maintain marketing because results are so important. I'd like to see if our services would be a good fit for your company.

ASK FOR NEXT STEP: I'd like to set up a phone meeting to start. Show you some samples. Learn about what you're doing. See where things may go from there. Can we do that?

Notes about the above Format A scripts

I said there are four and you counted three? The fourth is shown below.

Each of the above examples says something a bit different in Why You're Calling. The first one highlights maintenance and results. The second highlights a few of their services. The third incorporates all of those. Is one script going to be more effective than the others? Maybe.

Every group of prospects is a bit different, every person making calls is a bit different—put those together and the variables expand. The best way to find out what works best for you in your market is to experiment. At the very least, it helps to have a variety of scripts so you don't get bored.

Notice Richard asks for a phone meeting and positions it as a "start." Such a phone meeting makes it easy for he and the prospect to explore the fit at a general or high level. It's still a sales meeting, but with less commitment for both parties. (See the tip following Format B examples for more on this.)

Also, notice Richard still clearly states the core reason for his calls in his scripts: he wants a sales conversation. If he skipped this part he'd have an unstated agenda, which would undermine success. Prospects know he doesn't just want to show off some samples.

I'd also like to draw your attention to the phrase "I'd like to..." Richard says that twice—pretty close together. You may wonder if this kind of repeat sounds bad to prospects.

As long as the phrase is how you usually talk, most prospects won't notice. But if it bothers you, edit your script. Richard's might become: *"I'd like to see if our services would be a good fit for your company. Maybe we can start with a phone meeting. I can show you some samples..."*

While we're on word-smithing, you may wonder if "online" meeting would make more sense than "phone" meeting. I asked Richard about this and he explained he wanted the option to use phone and email rather than an online show and tell.

None of these scripts include Schedule. That's because it comes natural to Richard. The same applies to you, too. If you easily ask prospects for a good date and time—without any assumptive baloney—you don't need to include a reminder in your scripts. These scripts don't include Prep, either. Prep is totally optional.

Richard has been using a company name and "we" in his scripts. Let's switch things up a bit and show you an "I" example.

The fourth Format A

WHO YOU ARE: My name is Richard Sanderburg. I'm a marketing consultant.

WHY YOU'RE CALLING: I handle many kinds of marketing. Including social media and web based marketing. I focus on working with mid-size businesses. And emphasize helping clients maintain marketing because results are so important. I'd like to see if my services would be a good fit for your company.

ASK FOR NEXT STEP: I'd like to set up a phone meeting to start. Show you some samples. Learn about what you're doing. See where things may go from there. Can we do that?

TIP: "We" or "I" ~ Which is better?

This topic often generates lots of discussion about positioning, projecting a strong image, and so on. As fun as these discussions may be, they tend to focus on trying to somehow make prospects see us a certain way and these efforts backfire.

The truth is they both work well...as long as you focus on yourself rather than others. Choose the one you like best and feel free to change your mind (and scripts).

Revised Script: Format B

WHO YOU ARE: My name is Richard Sanderburg. I'm a consultant with ABC Marketing. My specialty is helping mid-size businesses make a big impression.

WHY YOU'RE CALLING: I'd like to give you a snapshot of our services and approach. And then see if you're interested in exploring a business fit.

ASK PERMISSION: Do you have a couple minutes?

GIVE INFORMATION: Let me start with the kinds of marketing we can handle. We can take care of everything from mail, to email, to interactive web marketing. We often handle branding for internal communiques. As well as newsletters. Clients tell us our approach is what sets us apart. Before we design and implement anything, we work on marketing strategy. That strategy includes how marketing will be maintained over time. Because that's how businesses get the most bang for their buck.

That's the snapshot (T). Of course, our services aren't necessarily a good fit for every organization. I'd like to see if they would be for yours.

ASK FOR NEXT STEP: Can we set up a meeting to do that?

SCHEDULE: Would you prefer to see me in person or talk things over on the phone?

PREP: I'd like to prepare for our meeting. Do you have time to answer three quick questions?

- Some people say their website is a good place for me to learn a bit about their business. Others, not so much. Shall I preview your site carefully or wait until we sit down together and talk?

- Any other online sources I should look at? Twitter? LinkedIn? Facebook page maybe?

- I can have some marketing samples ready to show you. What kind would you like to see?

Notes about the above Format B example

When Richard says Who he is, he mentions a specialty. Many people wonder if this is a best practice or if it is essentially required to grab attention.

Stating a specialty is certainly not required. Many prospects only half-hear what we say as we open a call, anyway. If you don't have a specialty, don't force it and don't worry about it.

If you have a specialty and it's important to you, go ahead and fold it into your script. But that doesn't mean you have to mention it when you say who you are, especially since the specialty might provide great content for Give Info.

Next, I'd like to draw your attention to how Richard covers two things in Why he's calling: He says what he'd like to do right now, in this moment and in this call (*"give you a snapshot"*). Richard also mentions the core reason for the call (*"exploring a business fit"*). It's important to say both of those things, otherwise there is an unstated agenda which will undermine success.

Also, notice the Why matches what's covered in Give Info. (If they didn't match, Richard should reword the Why because that's easier than rewording Give Info.)

The sentence structure and grammar in Give Info would make most English teachers cringe. However, the writing is well-suited for scripts—especially if they are my scripts. See the tip below about writing scripts in your own rhythm.

This example Format B includes some wording for Schedule because Richard found he was stumbling over that part. If he didn't need the reminder and guide, he could leave it out.

This example also includes Prep. As you can see, Richard doesn't just leap into the questions, he asks permission to ask some questions. This can be a good idea when using Format B because these calls take a bit longer.

If prospects don't give you permission to ask Prep questions that's not a bad sign, it usually means they don't have the time. When this happens, say something like, "Okay. I'll hold my questions for our meeting" and close the call.

Now let's consider the Prep questions themselves. Remember these are meant to help you prepare for a sales conversation, not segue into one.

Staying on the preparation side can be challenging. For example, most people look at a prospect's website to help prepare for a sales meeting. A marketing consultant like Richard is bound to take things further—he's going to analyze it. However, Richard's analysis shouldn't go too far. He needs more information and insight to do a good job, and he won't get those until the sales conversation.

Richard is well aware he should not jump ahead. He designed his Prep questions to orient how he should see the prospect's website and other online sources. Each prospect's responses will keep him from assuming there are things that should be fixed or that the prospect is happy with things as-is.

The prospect's answers to his first two questions may also provide hints about things they will want to talk about.

The third question shows a straight-forward example of what Prep is all about. Richard has a bunch of samples he *could* show prospects. Asking each prospect what they'd like to see helps him choose well.

Another Format B

WHO YOU ARE: My name is Richard Sanderburg. I'm a marketing consultant and specialize in helping mid-size businesses make a big impression.

WHY YOU'RE CALLING and ASK PERMISSION: Can I give you a snapshot of the kinds of services I provide. And then see where things may go from there?

GIVE INFORMATION: (Same as above.)

ASK FOR NEXT STEP: Of course, my services aren't necessarily a good fit for every organization. I'd like to see if they would be for yours. Can we set up a meeting to do that?

Notes about the above Format B

This example shows how Why You're Calling and Ask Permission can be blended. Let me parse the concepts and words out for you.

Remember that simply asking prospects if this is a good time doesn't work well. They need to know how you'd use that time.

Here is the sentence again: *"Can I give you a snapshot of the kinds of services I provide."* The "can I" asks permission. "Give you a snapshot" says how their time would be used.

Notice there is a period at the end of that sentence, not a question mark. That's because the entire properly-punctuated sentence would be:

"Can I give you a snapshot of the kinds of services I provide and then see where things may go from there?" This is a bit too long for a script so it was split in two.

This sentence is part of Why and Permission, too: *"And then see where things may go from there?"*

Remember Why You're Calling also needs to cover the core reason for your call: you'd like a sales conversation. But hold on...the line above does not state that clearly and directly. So what gives—did I just break my own rule? Yeah, that rule was at least bent a bit. Let's look at how the above phrase still retains a consultative approach.

A very handy phrase: "And then see..."

"And then see where things go from there" tells prospects there is more to your call than giving them a snapshot, overview, example, etc.

It is a very handy phrase because it fits well for many scripts, many markets, and many callers' styles. However, the phrase is not enough by itself. It has to be paired with a clear request for a sales conversation when you ask for the next step.

Create some space

Before Richard asks for a sales conversation he says, *"My services aren't necessarily right for every organization."*

This kind of statement works well on both ends of the phone line. He is not saying he assumes there is a good fit, he's saying he wants to see <u>if</u> there is such a fit. This reinforces the consultative message for prospects and keeps his feet on the ground at the same time.

Now for more tips relevant to the above examples.

TIP: More on we versus me

Solo business owners often wonder whether they should use "we" in their scripts. Will it make their business sound larger and more impressive? Will making a business appear larger bite them in the behind later?

Like many things in cold calling, the decision to use "we" versus "I" mostly depends on how you feel about it.

If you use "we" and feel like a fraud, that lack of confidence will probably hurt one way or another. Prospects may hear it in your tone or you may over-explain what "we" means. At the very least you'll feel uncomfortable as you make calls.

On the other hand, many solo practitioners have more of a "we" than they realize. If you have sub-contractors or people you can bring in when needed, you've got a "we."

However, if you use "we" because you're not confident about the benefits of working with you alone, step back and clarify those benefits. This is an important exercise whether you end up using "we" in your scripts or not.

TIP: Start with someone

No matter how accurate a list may be, there's no way to be sure the people you think you should ask for are the ones you most need to talk with.

Start with your best guess. If you are calling the wrong person, most people will tell you who you should call instead. This may occur as you start the call or as you ask for the next step.

When you're pointed in another direction, thank the first person and then call the person they directed you to. (And make a note on your list, of course.)

TIP: Find and write your rhythm

Most of the Format A and Format B examples in this book are based on scripts written by people who completed training. However, in adjusting these for the book they acquired a lot of Shawn flavor. The sentences in the scripts have commas where I would pause and periods where I would stop, but these may not work for you.

To learn to write scripts with your own rhythm:

Say the example scripts aloud a few times, pausing at commas and stopping for a breath at periods. If the script doesn't fit after practicing it my way a few times, rewrite the sentences. Put commas where you want to pause and periods where you want to stop.

Now say your version aloud a few times. Your goal is punctuation that helps you sound and feel like yourself. Make sure the sentences are not too long! Adjust as needed.

TIP: Start with a high level sales conversation

Instead of asking for a full and comprehensive sales conversation, you may want to start with a high level or general conversation on the phone. Here's why:

- These usually take less time, so they're easier to fit into your and your prospects' schedules.

- Keeping things at a high level involves less commitment, and prospects are often more willing to talk on this basis.

- There is less commitment for you, too, so you can afford to do less qualifying in cold calls. This is particularly helpful when your baseline involves things prospects rarely chat about with strangers who call out of the blue.

A high-level sales conversation on the phone is also a great first step when: selling includes discussing complex or personal issues, selling takes place over several conversations, selling involves many players.

Starting on the phone is also a great choice if your prospects seem to cancel a lot. These high-level phone meetings are easier to reschedule with less hassle for you.

High-level phone meetings are also dandy if you sell in places with bad traffic or when the weather makes it challenging to get to prospects.

If you're going to use these high-level sales conversations, you'll have to do it in an honest manner. If you try to use these as a foot in the door, most prospects will figure that out and you'll lose more opportunities than you gain.

Bad Example #3
Private Banker

This is Rochelle with Excalibur Bank. I'm a Banking Associate and part of the Wealth Management Services Group, which provides exclusive banking solutions to successful individuals such as yourself.

I'm aware you're busy so I'll keep this very brief. The reason for my call is to congratulate you on your recent nomination to the Boys and Girls Club board. I would also like to cordially invite you to our next open house. The event is on February 27 at 4 PM in our office. Charles Smith, one of our Bank Leaders, will speak on today's economy. You will also have opportunity to meet and talk with other Bank Leaders.

May I reserve one or two places for you?

What not to do, and why

"This is Rochelle with Excalibur Bank." That needs a comma (a pause), after she says her name.

"I'm a Banking Associate and part of the Wealth Management Services Group, which provides exclusive banking solutions to successful individuals such as yourself."

Say the above aloud and you'll recognize problem number one: the sentence is too long. Possible problem number two is the over-used "solutions."

The tone conveyed by the wording may or may not be problem number three. I need to cover a little background to explain why.

Private banking customers must meet a high minimum requirement for deposits and loans—it is indeed exclusive. Most private banking prospects have far more money than the bankers do. This sometimes makes bankers nervous, so they use overly-formal language or try to appeal to prospects' egos.

When we use language that doesn't reflect how we normally talk, it comes off as canned and feels uncomfortable. The same things happen when we promote aspects of a product or service we don't believe in.

The tone in this example works well if Rochelle values the exclusive nature of private banking and if she normally talks that way. Otherwise, this part of the script will flop on both ends of the phone line.

TIP: Rich people are still normal

The things that appeal to rich people are the same things that appeal to not-rich people. Those things fall into six benefit categories:

- Save money

- Increase money or value

- Peace of mind

- Convenience (save time or hassle)

- Enjoyment

- Image or ego

People who sell very expensive or exclusive products or services do not have to stick with image or ego benefits. Speaking as an ex-private-banker, I assure you selling based on convenience works very well, to name just one other benefit category.

In addition, the 'image or ego' benefit category does not necessarily equal expensive or conceited. This benefit category is a combination of the image projected by something and how we see ourselves (our self-image). Sure, "successful" and hints of "rich" land in this category but so do rebellious, practical, family-oriented, down to earth, thrifty, and so on.

We cannot accurately predict which benefit category will appeal to which prospect. Fortunately, talking about the benefits our clients value, backed-up by our own belief in that value, has strong general appeal.

Back to what not to do, and why

"...provides exclusive banking solutions to successful individuals such as yourself."

By saying, "individuals like yourself," Rochelle is telling prospects they qualify for private banking. This part of the script may dig her into a hole once she meets with prospects.

The problem is that prospects may only appear to qualify. Rochelle will have to back-peddle when they don't, making it harder to bring them into the regular part of the bank.

"I'm aware you're busy so I'll keep this very brief."

It's more effective to show respect for prospects' time by avoiding extra verbiage like that.

"The reason for my call is to congratulate you on your recent nomination to the Boys and Girls Club board. I would also like to cordially invite you to our next open house."

The nomination is what brought this prospect to Rochelle's attention. However, she is not primarily calling to extend congratulations and prospects know that.

In addition; the nomination may be old news, something that happened weeks or even months before it was publicized. (This is why applying what you find in research can be problematic.)

As for the invitation to the open house... There is more to this than socializing but in this case her prospects may *not* get that—they may not realize the open house is intended to be part of a sales process. And because Rochelle has not put the core agenda on the table, it may be harder to move from open house to an effective sales conversation.

"The event is on February 27 at 4 PM in our office. Charles Smith, one of our Bank Leaders, will speak on today's economy. You will also have opportunity to meet and talk with other Bank Leaders."

Rochelle's script capitalizes words that shouldn't be, which may prompt an odd inflection. Describing the speaker's topic is appropriate. But why would a prospect want to meet and talk with the others? That last sentence needs a benefit statement.

"May I reserve one or two places for you?" Ah, the classic and less effective assumptive close.

Introduction to the revised scripts

Private bankers and others often find prospects in articles about promotions, new jobs, nominations to boards, events, engagements, and so on. It's natural to want to include congratulations in calls but this presents challenges.

One challenge is managing the scripts. If you're going to include congratulations, your best bet is a separate script for each prospect. (Not one script with a blank where you insert the variable.) This takes more effort and the pay-off is questionable.

Another challenge is our own expectations. If we think extending congratulations will warm calls up, we will be disappointed.

Regardless, include congratulations only when you genuinely feel that way, otherwise your words will not ring true.

Bad verbal habits can be a challenge, too. Many people say they are calling *because of* an event, promotion, etc. You can avoid this error with good scripting.

The last challenge is the stalker effect. Some prospects forget or are unaware things have been announced. When we mention their promotion or attendance at a big event it seems slightly creepy to them. There's no way to avoid this entirely, so take it into account when deciding whether to include congratulations or not.

Our private banker, Rochelle, wants to extend congratulations and she's ready to deal with the challenges. This means the revised scripts are intended for one prospect: someone who has joined a board.

Revised Script: Format A

WHO YOU ARE: This is Rochelle, with the wealth management group of Excalibur Bank.

WHY YOU'RE CALLING: I'm calling for two reasons. One, I see you've joined the board of the Boys and Girls Club. Congratulations! I hear they do wonderful things. Two, I'd like to see if our banking services may be a good fit for you.

ASK FOR NEXT STEP: Can we arrange for a visit to our office to discuss that?

Notes about the above Format A

You may have noticed the phrase, *"I'm calling for two reasons."* Won't that sound as canned as "The reason for my call"?

Nope. What would sound canned is something like, "The reason for my call is I see you've joined the board..."

On the other hand, this won't work, either, "I see you've joined the board of the Boys and Girls Club. Congratulations! I hear they do wonderful things. I'd like to see if our banking services may be a good fit for you." That would definitely sound strange—what does one have to do with the other?

So if Rochelle wants to mention congratulations and the core reason for her call, she needs to tie them together. Saying she is calling for two reasons does that.

You may also notice the above script doesn't mention the open house. Including that would total three things and that's too many for Format A, which should be as concise as possible.

Revised script in Format B on the next page...

Revised Script: Format B

WHO YOU ARE: This is Rochelle, with the wealth management group of Excalibur Bank.

WHY YOU'RE CALLING: We're holding an open house. I'd like to tell you about the event and then see if you'd like to attend.

ASK PERMISSION: Is this a good time?

GIVE INFORMATION: Before I go further. I saw that you've joined the board of the Boys and Girls Club and want to say congratulations. I hear they do wonderful things. Now about our open house (T).

Our wealth management group provides private banking services. The open house gives people an opportunity to see our office. Meet the team, from tellers to lenders to bank leaders. Get a sense of who we are.

Our director, Charles Smith, will deliver a presentation about where we think the economy is headed. And how changes may impact our region. This is typical of the special programs we offer clients on a regular basis.

We hope this open house would be a first step to explore the fit between what you want from a bank and what we have to offer. It is on February 27th at 4 PM. We'll serve appetizers, wine and other refreshments.

ASK FOR NEXT STEP: Would you like to attend?

SCHEDULE: Would you like to bring any guests?

I'd like to send the details and a reminder. May I have your email?

TIP: What's the event really about?

Format B is perfect for inviting people to open houses, seminars and other events. There are three things to remember in this situation.

First: The objective of your call is to see if they want to attend and so that should be stated in Why You're Calling (along with saying you'd like to describe the event).

Second: If you want to lay a reasonable foundation for sales conversations, link the event to the buying experience on the prospect's end of things.

Is the event a practical demonstration of your expertise? A test-drive of what using the software would be like? A chance to meet the people who would provide service on a regular basis? (This example script has several links, including explaining that prospects would be able to come to other presentations if they were clients.)

The third thing to remember is this: if you're going to ask attendees for a sales conversation at or after the event, let them know upfront. In the above example:

"We hope this open house would be a first step to explore the fit between what you want from a bank and what we have to offer." Using "we hope" makes it clear you're not making assumptions, yet the sales issue is still in the open.

If you don't lay the sales issue out as part of the call, asking for a sales meeting at the event can seem sneaky—like you hid its real purpose.

Results can also suffer if the wording in your call, and later request for a sales conversation, are too subtle. Results are likely to be even worse if you wait to see if prospects ask you for a sales meeting.

All of that said, there is nothing horrible about holding events you hope will draw more prospects to you. Just keep the variables in mind as you create your script and event marketing plan, and be sure to set your own expectations accordingly.

More notes about the above Format B

Now I'd like to draw your attention to how the script extends congratulations. Here it is again: *Before I go further. I saw that you've joined the board of the Boys and Girls Club and want to say congratulations. I hear they do wonderful things. Now about our open house (T).*

There's a transition statement at the end, noted with the (T). *"Before I go further"* is actually a transition statement, too. That's how Rochelle smoothly goes into—and then out of—saying something that has nothing to do with the purpose of the call.

If you look at Give Info as a whole, you may see how easy it would be to copy the rest of the script and customize it for other prospects. That includes leaving congratulations out entirely.

Also notice that the date and time are shared toward the end of Give Info. This also serves as a transition to asking for the next step—no need to add one.

However, many callers prefer to cover date and time first because if there is a scheduling conflict they'd rather know early. If you take this approach, you may need a transition statement before you ask for the next step.

The last note about this example is a reminder that the goal is to see if prospects want to come to the event. That's why Ask for the Next Step is so direct.

Bad Example #4
List Provider

My name is Ralph Something.

(Name), I noticed you are the Vice President, Marketing within your company. I wanted to take a moment to introduce you to Best Bet Leads. We specialize in providing businesses with highly targeted business contacts in order to help them sell their products, services.

We have the unique ability to allow our customers to customize their contact list within specific industries, geographical areas, company departments, or even executive levels. (Name), you can even put together a list based on company size, revenue or Fortune rank. So whether you are trying to reach staff level contacts at small to mid-size companies, or corporate level executives at Fortune 500 giants, we can help.

(Name), to prove that we can provide you with the right contacts, we would like to extend to you 50 free highly targeted business contacts, with no commitment required. (Name), let's get started on that highly targeted list now.

What not to do, and why

The preceding fine example of what not to do came in as I worked on this section. What great timing! Thanks to some speedy typing, I was able to capture it almost word for word.

I couldn't see the actual script, of course. But based on how this fellow had to force sentences out and take quick breaths in weird places, the script was written using proper grammar. Poor guy.

Ralph's last name is not "something." It sounded like he said "Centerfield" but I'm not sure that was it, either.

I answer the phone using my name so he didn't have to ask for Shawn, he just leapt into the script.

"(Name), I noticed you are the Vice President, Marketing, within your company."

Um, wrong! That's a glaring error, considering Ralph is trying to sell me on his accurate lists.

However, callers working in many other industries make a similar error. In an effort to show prospects they did some research, many callers say something about the prospect's title, position or company. For example, "I see you have moved to new headquarters."

As Ralph illustrates, it's tough to know whether you have good information or not. The list says Vice President of Marketing but that may be wrong. The company's website or social media posts may promote their new HQ but that move may have occurred months ago.

Using information in that way also undermines success because it has no point—prospects know what their own title is.

"I wanted to take a moment to introduce you to Best Bet Leads."

An introduction. Is that all Ralph wants to do? Of course not. The unstated agenda undermines his credibility and annoys prospects at the same time.

"We specialize in providing businesses with highly targeted business contacts in order to help them sell their products, services."

Ralph continues to dig a hole by talking about the company's specialty of providing highly targeted lists just seconds after getting my title wrong. I'm harping on this to reinforce the point about using research in scripts: it easily and often backfires.

"We have the unique ability to allow our customers to customize their contact list within specific industries, geographical areas, company departments, or even executive levels."

The big problem in this sentence is the word "unique." The services Ralph describes are not even close to unique and most prospects know that. (VPs of Marketing certainly do.) Based on how overly-scripted Ralph sounded, the written sentence was probably also too long.

"(Name), to prove that we can provide you with the right contacts, we would like to extend to you 50 free highly targeted business contacts, with no commitment required."

Proactively making an offer to prove something is relatively rare so let's skip that part. Let's pretend Ralph just said, "Shawn, we would like to extend to you 50 free highly targeted business contacts, with no commitment required."

Is that why Ralph is calling me—he's got a quota of free samples to give out? Nope! In addition, Ralph sounded awkward. My hunch is that the wording was too formal for him, which added to the canned impression.

Now let's turn to "no commitment required." If getting a sample, demo or trial involve a commitment they are not genuine samples, demos or trials. Mentioning "no commitment" sounds mighty fishy.

"(Name), let's get started on that highly targeted list now."

This kind of assumptive close creates a lot of push-back. Ralph would have much greater success—with far less effort—if he simply asked if I wanted to sample the service. Better yet, Ralph should ask if I was interested in buying a list.

"(Name) (Name) (Name)"

I know Ralph had something like that in his script because he kept tossing my name in there. This, too, made him sound overly-scripted. If he didn't have such a youthful voice, it would also have come across as overly aggressive and slightly creepy.

TIP: No such thing as 100% accurate lists

I told the caller I was not interested but did not tell him why. He responded with several objection-handlers, including one about a guarantee of 100% accuracy.

When and if you shop for lists, run screaming away from providers who promise 100% accuracy. This promise is unrealistic and they know it. Should you try to get a refund based on that promise, you'll often get a run-around. (For more, see "How to shop for lists" in the marketing section of the Savage and Greene blog.)

Introduction to Ralph's revised scripts

This call was a marvelous example of how small errors can make a big, bad difference. Ralph didn't ask permission to use my time, he made a number of assumptions, he positioned the service as unique, the wording sounded awkward, and he used my name way too often.

On the other hand, the script has significant strengths. There are feature statements. There's a good description of the service. Ralph refers to "customers" before he uses "you." And, though he used it as an objection-handler (not shown), the free sample is customized for each potential customer.

If we put aside the part about 100% accuracy, there's a lot to work with for a Format B script. You might want to compare the revised versions to the original.

There are two example Format A scripts, and two Format B scripts.

Revised Script: Format A

WHO YOU ARE: My name is Ralph and I'm with Best Bet Leads. We are list brokers.

WHY YOU'RE CALLING: I'd like to see if we'd be a good list vendor for your company.

ASK FOR NEXT STEP: Can we set up a phone meeting to talk this over?

Another Format A

WHO YOU ARE: My name is Ralph and I'm with Best Bet Leads. We are list brokers.

WHY YOU'RE CALLING: I'd like to see if we'd be a good list vendor for your company. We offer a free customized sample list so you can really check us out.

ASK FOR NEXT STEP: Are you interested in evaluating our services?

Notes about the above Format A scripts

"Leads" can refer to lots of services, so the examples explain what Best Bet Leads does (list broker).

The company is not well-known, so Ralph could have left the name out and instead used something like, "My name is Ralph. I'm a list broker."

On the other hand, the company's real name is memorable so I gave it an equally-catchy fake name and included it. This, too, is a personal style thing—there's no right or wrong for using the company name or not.

The script uses "we are" instead of "we're." This is another style choice and you may want to see which would work best for you: Say the Who You Are part aloud a few times. Use "we are" and "we're" to see which is easier.

Both examples state the core reason for the call. The second one mentions the sample list, as well, which brings us to an important tip.

TIP: You're not selling samples

When you can offer samples, demos and so on, be sure you don't accidentally word your call as if that's what you sell. There are two things that will help you avoid this error.

One: Be very clear on the core reason for your call *and state that reason.*

e.g., You'd like to explore the business fit, you'd like a sales meeting, you'd like to be considered next time they roll out a RFP, you'd like to see if your services would provide value, etc.

Two: Get clear on what the sample, demo, portfolio review, analysis, etc. is for.

Start with its purpose and benefits on your side of the table. You're not necessarily going to share this with prospects so be as blunt and selfish as you want to.

- Portfolio or investment or retirement reviews help financial advisors see what kind of money and other assets there may be to work with. They also give advisors a chance to get a feel for working with the prospect.

  Reviews and analysis offer similar benefits for insurance brokers and bankers, to name just a couple others.

- Demos make sales easier because we can show prospects things rather than try to describe them.

  Interactive or hands-on demos often get prospects involved far more than discussion does.

- Showing samples often makes selling creative services much easier because prospects can say what they like and don't like. This, too, is often better than trying to uncover wants and needs using questions.

  The process also helps creative-service providers see what it may be like to work with the prospect.

Once you have clarity on how samples, demos or reviews may help you, think about how they may benefit <u>prospects</u>. For example:

- Portfolio reviews give prospects a chance to see what it would be like to work with an advisor.

  A fresh set of eyes and opinion may be beneficial, too. The same is true for insurance, and banking products and services.

  Note: If you go this route, avoid describing yourself as being like a doctor and/or the process as being a "second opinion." Both may evoke a negative image of illness.

- Being able to see how things work via a demo can be far more informative than reading about features and functions.

  When prospects can see exactly what they want to see and skip the rest, the benefits go up several notches because it saves time, too.

- Looking at samples of creative work is a demonstration of a provider's expertise and style.

  Seeing samples also makes it easier for prospects to explain what they're looking for and evaluate the provider's response.

Once you're clear on the purpose and potential benefits for each side of the table, decide whether you want to include mention of demo, samples, etc. in your call. If you do, it's often best to focus Give Info on this topic. There's an example in the second Format B below.

Revised Script: Format B

WHO YOU ARE: My name is Ralph and I'm with Best Bet Leads. We are list brokers.

WHY YOU'RE CALLING: We'd like to see if we can earn your business. I'd like to introduce our services. And then see where things might go from there.

ASK PERMISSION: Do you have a minute?

GIVE INFORMATION: We provide highly targeted business contacts. Our goal is to help customers sell their products and services. Lists can be customized for industries, geographic area, department type, company size or revenue level. Customers can even put together lists based on executive level or rank in the Fortune 500.

In a nutshell. Whether you're trying to reach contacts at small companies. Or C-suite executives at the giants, we can help (T).

ASK FOR NEXT STEP: There are many list brokers out there. We'd like to earn your business. Are you interested?

Notes about the above Format B example

One of the things missing in the original script was mention of the core reason for the call. Another big problem was failing to show respect for prospects' time by asking permission.

The revised versions (there's another one below) fix those problems. If you compare them to the original, I think you'll also see a higher level of professionalism and confidence. By adding respect for prospects, the call stands out from its competition in a good way.

In the above example, Give Info changed a word here and there and adjusted punctuation of the original. Sometimes that's all it takes to make scripts more effective.

One of the things retained from the original is how Ralph mentioned "customers" before he said, "you." See the tip below to learn why this can help prevent push-back.

I'd also like to draw your attention to the paragraph which ends with a "(T)." That whole paragraph is actually a transition statement and if it wasn't part of a script it would be just one sentence: "In a nutshell, whether you're trying to reach contacts at small companies or C-suite executives at the giants, we can help."

You may also notice there's no mention of the free sample. That's because the free sample is not the point of the call. This doesn't mean Ralph shouldn't talk about the free sample at all. In fact, it may deserve center stage. I'll show you an example of this in a bit.

TIP: "You" backs prospects into a corner

YOU can do this, YOU can do that, here's how it benefits YOU...

Even though we may use it in a general way, prospects tend to hear "you" as an assumption about their individual wants and needs. Many don't want to let such assumptions stand for fear it will be taken as agreement. This is too much of a commitment and—feeling backed into a verbal corner—many prospects push right back.

The way to avoid these problems is to talk about customers or types of customers in general terms (e.g., "People" and "HR managers"). This also sends a message the prospect's peers use and value the products or services.

All of that noted, it's not necessary to avoid using "you" altogether.

Another script in Format B on the next page...

Another Format B

WHO YOU ARE: My name is Ralph and I'm with Best Bet Leads. We are list brokers.

WHY YOU'RE CALLING: We know there are lots of list providers out there. I'd like to describe how people can test our services. And then see where things might go from there.

ASK PERMISSION: Do you have a couple minutes?

GIVE INFORMATION: Thanks. We specialize in providing highly targeted contact lists. To show the value of our service, we give potential clients a list of 50 contacts at no charge. This free sample list is customized for industry, location, company size. It can be customized based on revenue level or even job title. That's just some of the data available.

You can even use our online form to define the sample list at your convenience. We'd set up a time to talk at some point after you do that. That's how the test-drive would work (T).

ASK FOR NEXT STEP: Are you interested in seeing if we'd be the right list provider for your business?

SCHEDULE: Let's set a time for me to call you. I know you need time to define your list and take a look at it. When should we plan to discuss things?

Notes about the above Format B

Let's start with several points about Why You're Calling.

This example acknowledges there are lots of list brokers out there. This kind of flat statement is often enough to prevent objections from prospects who have a someone or something they're satisfied with (i.e., they have a list broker).

Ralph also tells prospects how he'd like to use their time in this call—he wants to describe something. And, instead of making the call about the sample itself, it is about the purpose of the sample as a way to test their services.

This example Why does not specifically mention the core reason for the call. This one uses *"and then see where things might go from there."* This approach works well as long as you also clearly state the core reason at some point in the call. In the above example, the core reason is part of Ask for the next step. Instead of asking prospects if they'd like to get a sample list, the Ask focuses on *"seeing if we'd be the right list broker for your business."*

Now let's touch on Give Info. This example mentions a specialty (highly targeted lists) to emphasize the nature of the sample. Give info describes a handful of ways the sample can be customized but keeps it brief.

Also notice the mention of an online form. Let me explain how that ended up in this Format B.

One of the objection-handlers the real caller used mentioned various ways prospects could get their sample list, including an online form. Based on the way he went on and on about this, I'm pretty sure lots of prospects say they don't have time to figure out what kind of list they'd want and therefore they don't want a sample.

One of Format B's strengths is you can use Give Info to prevent common objections like that. In my revised script, Give Info nips the no-time objection in the bud by mentioning the online form prospects can use *"at your convenience."* (See the tip below for more on this.)

I'd also like to draw your attention to how the script mentions setting a time to talk after the prospect gets the sample list. This helps reinforce the idea the sample is meant to be part of exploring the business fit. This approach isn't magic, of course, some prospects will still take the sample and run.

This Format B includes Schedule and applies a best practice of giving prospects control. Instead of telling prospects when you'll call, ask them to give you a time. This is yet another thing that helps develop a good relationship from the start. Having prospects set the appointment also reduces cancellations. All in all, you'll get there faster if you let the prospect drive.

TIP: Prevent objections in Give Info

You can prevent many common objections by defusing the issues in Give Info.

Start by creating a list of objections you often get when calling. Add objections you get when selling (because prospects often have these objections when you call them—they just don't express them).

Next, identify how you can handle each objection and translate that into your scripts.

Here are examples:

A printing company likes to promote its "green" process. Many prospects prefer to work with such a printer but also think it costs more. Rather than avoid promoting the environmentally-friendly aspects, the printing company's reps include the following in Give Info:

"We're very proud of our green printing processes and high quality materials. Clients often tell us they shopped around and were surprised to find our rates are very competitive."

Credit unions have a reputation for the personal touch. On the other hand, lots of their members (customers) do not know they offer sophisticated products and services. Callers from one of these credit unions include this simple statement in Give Info:

"We offer the same range of products and services the big banks do."

The marketing consultant whose scripts we saw earlier runs into objections from prospects who like doing their marketing and believe they're good at it. To prevent these silent objections, Give Info includes:

"Some of our clients prefer to delegate all or most of the marketing to us. Others put just some of the marketing on our plate. Often the tasks that take too much time or require certain expertise."

A banker realizes the bank she works for has a reputation for high turnover. From the prospects' perspective, a change in bankers would create inconvenience. Rather than promise she'd stay—which most prospects won't believe anyway—the banker includes this in Give Info:

"I am just part of a team. I always introduce my colleagues to potential customers. So they know who would ensure excellent service continues even if I move on."

That's just a few examples of how Give Info content can help prevent objections.

The last bad example gets its own chapter because it may be extra important to readers...it's all about what not to do when mailing something and then calling.

The Wrong Way To Mail And Then Call

THIS BAD EXAMPLE gets a special introduction because it focuses on one of the most common ways people try to "warm" calls up: by mailing stuff and then calling.

Mailing first does not improve calling results. It does not make people more prone to taking your call. It does not inspire more people to set sales appointments, nor does it increase sales.

However, there is a nugget of truth in thinking mailing and calling work well together. You see, when you use two complementary marketing tools within the same general period of time to the same pool of prospects, your overall total response rate is often higher.

That's not because letters warm up calls or vise-versa, it's because you're increasing the chance of capturing attention. Some people will answer the phone, some won't. Some people will look at the mailer, some won't. By using two tools that work well together, you have a greater chance more prospects in total will respond.

The mailer warm-up myth not only creates unrealistic expectations, it drives a common counter-productive mistake: making the call <u>about</u> the item mailed. The bad script is an example of this, but I want to help you drop the myth from your brain before I show the example.

Instead of mailing things and making calls, imagine you buy billboard space and radio ads. These are two other marketing tools that complement—they work well together.

The billboards go up first. Picture that billboard. Maybe it's got an innovative tagline and a striking photo or image. Got it pictured?

Now the radio ads start running. Do those ads say, "Did you see the billboard? Did you read the billboard? Do you have any questions about the billboard?"

No they do not, because that would be weird. The same is true for mailing and calling. Linking them together seems just as strange to prospects and that's only one reason why those calls backfire (I'll cover more reasons in a bit).

Key point: Instead, each marketing item should stand on its own. The mailer should stand on its own. The calls should stand on their own. Do not link the mailer to the calls or the calls to the mailer, especially in your head.

Now for the bad example. This is the last one of Contact/Prospect scripts and it came from one person who managed to make pretty much every mistake you can in this situation, and then some.

Bad script example #5

Hello. My name is Sydney and I'm with the downtown office of ABC Bank. How are you today?

The reason for my call is to follow up on the letter I sent you last week. I know you're very busy, as am I, but did you perhaps have a chance to read it? Do you have any questions?

Well, as described in the letter, your company can improve its efficiency considerably by doing your banking without leaving your office.

Our "FLEXONLINE" bypasses the need to physically deposit checks in the branch and that's only one way this product meets your banking needs.

I would like to set up a no obligation 15 minute appointment to show you "FlexOnLine." In fact, I'll be in your area on ___. When would be a good time to drop by?

What not to do, and why

"Hello. My name is Sydney and I'm with the downtown office of ABC Bank. How are you today?"

By now you may recognize two problems. Reading "Hello" is likely to make it sound a bit off. The dreaded "How are you?" will pull results down, too. On the positive side, she kept her name and company separate.

"The reason for my call is to follow up on the letter I sent you last week. I know you're very busy, as am I, but did you perhaps have a chance to read it? Do you have any questions?"

That "reason for my call" will make Sydney sound—and probably feel—awkward.

She also says that reason is a follow up...on what? She wants to make sure the post office delivered the letter? No, wait, she wants to check on prospects' reading habits; and of course answer questions because prospects hate to walk around with questions in their head.

Sheesh. So far, Sydney has not expressed the real reason for her call and this will annoy most prospects.

In addition, there's some strange wording in there. Many callers say, "I know you're busy" but Sydney adds, "as am I." That's fine if she normally talks that way, but chances are high this proper grammar is not natural and will sound a bit weird.

This script also illustrates another reason why tying calls to mailers backfires. This script puts Sydney at the mercy of prospects. She is stuck if they didn't receive the letter, don't remember it, didn't read it, or don't have questions.

"Well, as described in the letter, your company can improve its efficiency considerably by doing your banking without leaving your office."

If something was described in the letter, why repeat it in the call? Also notice Sydney implies the prospect's company is inefficient.

"Our 'FLEXONLINE' bypasses the need to physically deposit checks in the branch and that's only one way this product meets your banking needs."

This sentence is too long for a script. Sydney uses a product name, which may not be a good idea. She also put the product name in quotes and all-caps, which is definitely not a good idea because either of those things may prompt her to say the name differently than the rest of the sentence. If she does, she'll sound like she's reading a script.

TIP: Using product or service names

The guidelines for product or service names are similar to those for company names.

- If a product/service is well known (in a good way), use the name.

- If the name says what it does, use it.

- If neither of those apply: if you use the name, describe what the product or service does. (Or leave the name out altogether so the script is more concise.)

There's one other guideline to consider for product, service and company names:

- You may want to use them if they are particularly catchy. Just be sure to describe the product or service, too.

If you include product or service names in your script, do not put the name in quotation marks. Do not use all-caps, even if that's the way the name is usually shown.

In Sydney's original script, she actually included the registered trademark symbol next to the product name. This is the only time I've seen this but in case it needs to be said: don't do that. Including symbols adds a tiny visual distraction, which makes a script less effective as a guide. Now, back to ripping apart this classic counterproductive script.

Back to what not to do, and why

"I would like to set up a no obligation 15 minute appointment to show you 'FLEXONLINE.' In fact, I'll be in your area on ___. When would be a good time to drop by?"

Again with the good old 15 or 20 minute appointment. Could this script be any more trite? Why, yes, it can! Because Sydney will magically be in each prospect's area!

Most prospects will see right through this technique and decline the appointment. However, this approach can also set up a problem with prospects who do agree to appointments. What happened for the real caller illustrates this problem perfectly.

In real life, a handful of prospects told Sydney to come on by and give them a demo. She did that, thought she and the prospects had good conversations, and came back to her branch believing most of them would buy.

When Sydney later called these prospects, none of them wanted to open accounts and sign up for the product—but that's not the worst part. She was shocked to hear a few of them say things like this, "Oh, yeah, it looked great. Called my bank to see if they have the same thing and I'm all set." What! How did that happen?

Here's how: Sydney did not ask for a sales conversation, she asked to show prospects the product. This laid an extremely weak foundation for the meeting.

When Sydney and I talked about the script and what happened with these prospects, I learned the above error was compounded twice. As she started each demo, Sydney again said the purpose was to show prospects the nifty product.

And then, after the demo, she failed to ask prospects if they wanted to open an account and sign up for the product. Instead she asked, "What do you think?" This indirect approach undermined success at each key point.

This situation may seem unusual. It's not. Prospects don't necessarily have a sales mindset. They agree to see demos because they're curious. They agree to let reps introduce themselves because they're nice. And they agree to meet because the caller manages to make "in the area" sound genuine.

TIP: Make it a clear ask

If you don't ask for a sales conversation, you don't necessarily have agreement for a sales conversation. Put the core reason for your call front and center, and make the request in clear language. That's the only way you'll know where you stand.

Revised Script: Format A

WHO YOU ARE: My name is Sydney and I'm with the downtown branch of ABC Bank.

WHY YOU'RE CALLING: We have a new product that lets business owners handle more banking without having to leave the office. I'd like to show it to you and see if this opens the door to earning some of your business.

ASK FOR THE NEXT STEP: Are you open to considering us as a potential bank?

SCHEDULE: It's a hands-on demo. Most people I meet with spend up to 45 minutes. Gives us time to go over the features you may find most useful. And discuss a possible fit for us as one of your banks. What would be a good time for you?

PREP: Do you have an office manager or others who handle some of the banking? If you do, I'd like to be able to show them the demo, too.

Notes about the above Format A

Notice how briefly and concisely the above script covers the product. If you use a product focus in Format A, you'll have to do the same.

Also notice the core reason for the call is clearly stated using *"and see if this opens the door to earning your business."* This is reinforced by clearly asking for a next step sales conversation—not just a demo—which sets a solid foundation for sales conversations.

This example includes Schedule because Sydney wants enough time for a good demo and conversation. Rather than hoping prospects will give her enough time once she gets there, she asks for a certain amount. She uses "most people" to add credibility and positions a benefit for the amount (go over features the prospect may find most useful).

You might have also noticed the above example mentions a potential fit as "one of your banks"; meaning ABC is not trying to get all their business. See the tip below for more about this approach.

This particular Prep uses just one question and it's rhetorical. That only works because of the statement that follows it. The next Format A example shows a direct way to ask the same thing. The next example also shows how to safely mention something mailed earlier.

Another Format A

WHO YOU ARE: My name is Sydney and I'm with the downtown branch of ABC Bank.

WHY YOU'RE CALLING: We'd like the opportunity to earn your business. We have a new product that lets people handle more banking without having to leave their shop or office. Sent a brochure earlier this week. I'd like to give you a hands on demo. And see if this opens a door to becoming one of your banks.

ASK FOR THE NEXT STEP: Can we set up a demo and discussion?

SCHEDULE: I'd like 45 minutes or so. Gives us time to go over the things you want to see and discuss a possible business fit at the same time. What time would be good for you?

PREP: Do you have an office manager or others who handle banking and should see the demo?

Notes about the above Format A

Why starts—and ends—with stating the core reason for the call. Without these, the Ask would be weak.

Why also mentions—just flatly mentions—a brochure mailed earlier. Though there's little to no value in tying calls to mailers, many people really, really, really want to say something. The example shows how to do that and avoid mail/call mistakes.

Schedule uses less formal wording. Prep uses a direct question.

Some people may see this example as one that will sound more confident than the earlier example. Others may see this one as less professional. Either of those impressions may be right...or wrong.

The key issue is not how prospects might hear the script. The key issue is how the script suits your natural way of talking. The more you write the way you talk, the better results you'll have.

TIP: More than one may be wonderful

Many people prefer to have more than one bank, broker, financial advisor, printer, tech support service, etc. Even more people are reluctant to give a new provider all of their business right from the start.

However, many service-providers prefer to be the one and only. Bankers like to have all of a customer's accounts, insurance brokers want to get that Broker of Record designation, etc. Prospects often know this and hesitate to agree to a sales conversation because they don't want to deal with it.

As shown in these examples, one way to defuse that issue is to break the image by saying, "one of..." your banks, brokers, advisors. This only works well if you mean it; and so if you truly prefer to be the one and only, do not fudge this in cold calls.

Format B example on next page...

Revised: Format B Script

One of the advantages of using the mail is you can include descriptive information, such as product brochures. Format B lets you do the same thing.

WHO YOU ARE: My name is Sydney. I'm a business banker with ABC Bank. I'm on first avenue, in our downtown branch.

WHY YOU'RE CALLING: We'd like the opportunity to earn your business. We have a new product with a number of time-saving functions. I'd like to tell you about just one of those. And then see where things may go from there.

ASK PERMISSION: Do you have a minute or two?

GIVE INFORMATION: Thanks. Banking products and services have definitely advanced since I started years ago as a teller. Helping our customers save time has advanced, too. And that's what this product is about.

One time-saving feature is remote deposit of checks. That's been around for a while now but it had limitations. One problem for many of our customers was the limit on items deposited that way. We worked with our vendors to meet that challenge.

In our product, the number of items is customized to each business and can easily be adjusted. For example, the number can be increased in advance of a busy season. One of my clients had a hugely successful week and needed an increase right away. She gave us a call and it was done.

That's just one of the features of this product (T). A demo does it more justice. I'd be happy to come to your shop and show you.

ASK FOR NEXT STEP: If you're open to considering ABC as your bank, I'd like to set up a meeting. What do you say?

Notes about the above Format B

Before going any further, I should clarify I made up the product feature. Maybe it doesn't actually exist, maybe it's old hat—just go with it.

In the above example script, Sydney added "business banker." That's not her official title, it is a concise way to share title and specialty at the same time.

The script also mentions a more specific branch location. This may come in handy when calling business prospects in that area. On the other hand, she may want to leave it out when calling prospects who are out of the area.

Ask Permission mentions a minute "or two." The call won't actually take two minutes, this is just how Sydney talks and her scripts should follow that.

Notice the Why begins with the core reason for the call. For comparison, here is a version without that statement:

"We have a new product with a number of time-saving functions. I'd like to tell you about just one of those. And then see where things may go from there."

The above version of Why puts more reliance on the product itself and there are pros and cons to this. On the upside, it can be effective because it makes the topic of calls more concrete. On the downside, a product focus can be too narrow—there may not be enough interest in that particular product.

There is no right or wrong here. Results vary from market to market, and can depend on the product or service itself. If you want to test drive a product or service focus; go for it and see what happens.

Give Info begins with "Thanks" to remind Sydney to say it. Once she gets used to it, she should delete the word from her scripts.

You may have also noticed this script reveals Sydney's been in banking for a while and started as a teller. Will prospects care?

Some will, some won't. It's important to Sydney and so including it lets more of her personality shine through, which will definitely help increase the level of success with calls.

This script includes a couple examples of exactly how one of the product features (adjusting number of checks deposited) may apply. This is more effective than just mentioning features by themselves.

TIP: Why examples and stories work well

Using examples, or telling a story about how customers use a feature, is much more powerful than simply describing the feature. Some prospects may personally relate, but that's not why examples, stories and benefit statements are so effective. Here's the scoop:

Remember that most prospects are not giving you their full attention. They're not necessarily rude or completely uninterested—distraction is just part of their environment. In addition, the topic of your call is just a small piece of their work or personal life. It's a large part of your work and you understand the value of features, but that's not true for most prospects.

Examples, stories and benefit statements mean prospects don't have to make the connections on their own, and you don't have to hope they pay more attention than usual.

Back to notes

The transition statement in the above example is, *"That's just one of the features of this product."* This statement signals a switch in direction of what Sydney is saying. Signaling makes it easier for prospects to make that change, too.

I also want to draw your attention to how Sydney Asks for the next step. She says, *"If you're open to considering ABC as your bank, I'd like to set up a meeting. What do you say?"*

This Ask loops back to the core reason for the call: she wants to earn their business. It's also clear she's not asking to give them a demo, she's asking for a sales meeting that happens to include a demo.

The remaining notes for this example script are more about what is missing.

One thing that's missing is a spotlight on the demo. In this script the demo plays a much smaller part. That's because the demo covers just one product the bank offers, it's not a demo meant to show off the bank's value as a whole.

Let's flip that situation over: when a demo or sample is meant to demonstrate value as a whole, give the demo/sample center stage and use Give Info to describe it. Include a description of how the demo or sample would work, how participating may benefit prospects, and anything prospects would need to do on their end.

Another thing missing from this script is wording like "we aren't the right bank for every business." Instead, Sydney implies that if the prospect wanted to become a customer she'd be all for it. This approach is only appropriate when calling prospects you have pre-qualified, and when you know you'd like their business. See the next section on qualifying for more on this.

Key Scripting Points, and Next

The content of your Contact/Prospect scripts will be used in your other scripts. There are two formats, cleverly titled "Format A" and "Format B."

Format A gets right to the central point of your call: you'd like to have a sales conversation. Work on this format first, even if you don't think you'll actually use it. Doing so provides important practice with the hard part and makes drafting the other scripts much easier.

The powerhouse for Format B is Give Information. In that part, you provide information to prospects (instead of trying to dig it out of them). This often sparks interest where there was none, helps build relationships, and can prevent objections—to name just a few things.

Learning to write good scripts is as important as using them. Writing scripts is different from other writing. Sentences should be shorter. Punctuation should be simple: commas and periods. Grammar should be tossed out of the window—we don't talk that way.

Write using wording that sounds like the regular you; that is, the you while at work, feeling confident and comfortable.

Apply the tips sprinkled throughout this section so you can avoid common problems.

Both Format A and Format B have their pros and cons. Each of them are effective. Some callers have a favorite they use most often, some callers use both. I recommend creating scripts using both formats, and then using each so actual experience guides your choice.

Format B has one advantage over Format A: it can be used to qualify prospects. Let's take a thorough look at qualifying and how to use it.

QUALIFYING

Often it isn't the mountains ahead that wear you out,
it's the little pebble in your shoe.

(Muhammad Ali)

Qualifying and a Catch-22

REMEMBER THE THINGS people do not like about getting cold calls? Being asked questions is on that list. There are several reasons why we find questions annoying. Some questions seem insincere. Some are slightly manipulative, inane, or both.

Many questions seem selfish on the caller's part. They're all about whether prospects are worth their time and effort—and this is why qualifying can be challenging.

As callers using a consultative approach, we want to demonstrate respect for prospects but we don't want to waste our time, either. Achieving the right balance is about managing the line between prospecting and selling.

Remember: Selling doesn't begin unless and until the prospect has agreed to evaluate the fit. (Giving permission to continue with a call is not the same thing.) To explain how qualifying when prospecting differs from qualifying when selling, I'll begin with the latter.

Qualifying when selling

When we're *selling*, qualifying deals with many topics, and does so at a deep level.

Topics include the prospect's wants, needs, interests, perspective, priorities, concerns, and so on. Our general goal for these topics is to explore the fit between what we offer and what the prospect wants and needs.

Qualifying when selling also includes these topics: timing, decision process and players, budget, and control over budget. Our general goal here is more about what the prospect has to offer us, as well as uncovering any obstacles may be in the way of a sale.

There is only one way to qualify effectively when selling: by asking direct questions. The prospect's answers to qualifying questions drives how the sale proceeds, including when and if we ask for their business. (For more, see "Don't guess, qualify" in the Selling section of the Savage and Greene blog.)

Why sales-qualifying backfires in cold calls

When we ask sales-qualifying questions in cold calls we're attempting to jump ahead, and so many prospects push back.

In addition, the information we manage to get tends to be low quality. Prospects tell us very little or even give misleading answers (sometimes because they just want to get us off the phone). To avoid those problems, we need to qualify differently.

Qualifying when prospecting

When cold calling, qualifying focuses on very high level or basic issues. The topics are things that define whether you ask for a sales conversation or not: period.

There are two ways to qualify when cold calling: by asking direct questions, or by describing baseline qualifiers. Format B is perfect for either approach but before we look at examples we need to tackle two things. Do you *really* need to qualify? If you do need to qualify, on what exactly?

Do you really need to qualify?

When cold calling, qualifying drives whether we ask for that next step sales appointment or not. That's all. That's it.

So take a minute to think about the things you already know about your prospects before you pick up the phone to call them. For example:

Maybe you already know the company meets a basic size requirement because you see that information in a reliable database.

Perhaps you know they meet account balance minimums because you can actually see some of their account information.

Maybe experience with existing clients tells you these prospects probably use—or could use—products and services like yours. (This is a common situation.)

In cases like the above, you already know prospects meet your basic requirements. This means the only information you really need to uncover is whether they're open to having a sales conversation.

In other words: you don't need to qualify, you only need to ask for the next step.

Mini-lecture on qualifying

Does the above make sense? Great! But you still need to be careful once you get on the phone.

Sometimes people embrace qualifying guidelines on paper, and then when they reach prospects willing to chat they want to use the "opportunity" to dig in. Don't do that without clear agreement from the prospect: ask for a sales conversation.

Mini-lecture over. It's time to turn to what happens when you do need to qualify:

- How do you determine your basic requirements?
- How do you raise the issues and prevent pushback at the same time?

As usual, it helps to analyze the other guys.

The Other Guys' Qualifying

THIS CHAPTER COULD have been a very long one because the list of questions people think they should ask to qualify is long. For example, a class of about twenty sales reps often collectively come up with over fifty different questions!

As always, I'll show you real questions from real people. However, to keep this chapter's length in check, I'll just show typical questions within common categories.

Even though I've honed things down you may still notice some overlap. This illustrates how we end up asking questions that seem annoyingly repetitive to prospects.

The examples also mix B2C and B2B. This is partly because the qualifying topics and errors are the same, and partly because all prospects are human. Let me explain...

A business question is still a question

Callers often think business questions won't bother prospects. After all, they're executives, managers and owners and they'll appreciate we want to get down to it, right?

Wrong. Most prospects find business-oriented questions just as invasive and annoying as personal questions.

I want to emphasize it's not just the number of questions that causes problems, it's also who's asking. We callers are strangers. We're interrupting. We're on the phone, which adds to the slight sense of invasion. All of this means we need to choose qualifying questions carefully.

Choosing questions wisely

To choose qualifying questions wisely, we must consider three things:

- Is the information so basic we can probably get it in other ways before we call?

- Would the prospect's answer really make a difference in whether we ask for a sales conversation?

- Is this the right time to try to discuss it, or will asking now create too many problems?

Keep those factors in mind as we look at potential qualifying questions.

How the example questions are organized

Picture a group of people representing a wide variety of businesses. They have a mix of prospects, too: some call B2B and some call B2C.

They start by brainstorming questions they think they want to ask (or "should" ask). Next, they organize the questions into categories. There are a ton of questions but they end up fitting into three categories.

Some questions ask about the same thing but use different wording. The duplicates are deleted, reducing the list of questions in each category.

Got the picture? Now we'll analyze each example question to see if it's a keeper or not.

Questions about details and timeframes

I'm showing detail-oriented questions first because many callers want to ask these first.

"How many employees do you have?"

That is a qualifying question if we're selling something that involves a minimum or maximum number of employees. However, this kind of information may be easily found elsewhere; if so, it should not be asked.

"How many employees work 20 hours or more per week?"

That is a stronger qualifying question because that sort of detail may not be easily found in advance. However, many prospects will find it invasive and shut down a bit, so the issue is whether we truly need this detail now.

"Do you have any training initiatives planned for the next three months for which elearning is an option?"

"Do you have IT projects planned within the next three months that you also plan to outsource?"

Both of those questions involve a timeframe set by the caller (or their boss). The idea is to find prospects with projects in the near term, perhaps to avoid "wasting" time on other prospects.

The downside: prospects rarely offer information beyond what they're asked. This means the caller will probably miss out on opportunities outside of that stated timeframe; e.g., four months.

Key point: A specific timeframe may exclude too many prospects.

The above examples also illustrate something else to consider: many people who engage training and elearning services would find the above question self-centered—almost rude. In contrast, a lot of IT managers are used to a question with a timeframe. They tend to see it as an approach that doesn't waste their time.

Key point: Your target market affects what will and will not work for qualifying.

"Are you planning to sell your business within the next five years?"

That question includes yet another timeframe. It's also potentially touchy because selling a business is often a stressful matter.

On the other hand, few business owners have any sort of timeframe attached to the idea of selling their business so using one probably narrows qualifying too much.

Key point: Asking about a touchy issue, or one prospects rarely think about, is not effective. All in all, that kind of question may need to be tossed.

"Do you plan to retire within the next five years?"

Financial advisors and planners like to ask that kind of question. It is yet another question that is narrow and overly-personal—and there's one more reason why it's likely to backfire.

Financial advisors and planners are in the business of helping people figure out when and if they can retire. Asking questions which put that onus on prospects undercut the caller's position as an expert guide.

Key point: If you are in the business of helping clients answer certain questions, don't ask them as qualifiers.

The above question can also generate significant backlash if asked at the wrong time. For example, many people who had hoped to retire during the latest recession were forced to put that aside for years. Woe to the caller who asked them the above question at that time!

Key point: Embrace new realities and adjust your approach to qualifying.

"Do you have an office manager who handles banking or do you have to do it all yourself?"

Would the answer determine whether you ask for a sales meeting or not? No, and so that is not a qualifying question.

"Do you spend at least $35,000 per year on direct marketing?"

"Is your non-401K investment portfolio worth at least $75,000?"

Answers to the above questions may indeed define whether we ask for a sales conversation or not. Alas, few prospects are willing to answer because these essentially ask, "Are you worth my effort?" Including a dollar amount also increases the invasion factor.

In sum: Those two questions stay on the qualifying list. I'll show you how to deal with the challenges in a bit.

"Is your household income over $175,000?"

That kind of question often looks like a qualifier because it's part of a description of a target market. But that's the problem—it's just part of the picture.

Take private bankers, for example. Their typical client has household income of at least $175,000. But the bottom line is how much prospects keep in their bank accounts. Let's swap the above for *"Do you generally keep over $25,000 in your bank accounts?"*

Key point: Qualify for the bottom line issues.

"Who makes decisions about...?"

That question should not be asked in cold calls. It insults the person you're speaking with and jumps the gun into selling.

Questions about feelings

This next set is full of excellent questions asked at the wrong time. Not one of them is effective for qualifying when cold calling.

"How confident are you that you can retire when ready?"

"Do you know that nearly 80% of businesses have too much or too little insurance?"

"Would you say your direct marketing is effective, or tossing things at a wall to see if something sticks?"

"Has someone in your family needed long term care? How did it affect them?"

Questions like those are intended to uncover "pain," be intriguing, and make prospects think. They accomplish the thinking part, alright, as in, "What the heck?"

Do not use those kinds of questions to qualify. If the topic or message is important to you, leverage Give Information to put it on the table in a powerful way.

Questions about the current what or whomever

This set consists of more misleading questions—they only appear to be good for qualifying. See if you can figure out what the callers hope to uncover.

"Who is your current insurance carrier?"

"When was the last time your banker called you without a sale in mind?"

"Do you have a marketing consultant?"

"How long have you used your CPA?"

"Are you happy with your...?"

Those questions are a roundabout way to try to find out whether a prospect is open to considering a potential replacement. They don't work because the answers will not actually address that issue. For example, just because someone has used the same CPA for five or ten or fifteen years, that doesn't mean they are or are not open to change.

The best way to find out if prospects are open to considering us is to ask: ask for a next-step sales conversation.

What's left?

Of the example questions, the most viable for qualifying are:

- Number of employees working 20 hours or more per week?

- Do they spend at least $35,000 per year on direct marketing?

- Investment portfolio worth at least $75,000?

- Keep at least $25,000 in accounts?

- IT projects within the next three months they plan to outsource?

That is just five out of twelve questions, which is typical. We often start with a long list and need to whittle it down.

How to find your qualifying issues

Before I show you simple steps for identifying your qualifiers, let's review some key concepts. Focus on what you need to know to determine whether you'll ask for that sales conversation. Remember it's about what you <u>need</u> to know, not what would be nice to know. Asking for the sales conversation may be the only qualifier you need.

To find your qualifying issues:

- Create a list of questions you think you want to ask and/or "should" ask. Brain-dump all of them onto paper.

- Evaluate each question by itself, one by one. Would a prospect's answer make a difference, or would you ask for a sales conversation regardless?

    If a prospect's answer would define whether you ask for the next step, that's a qualifying issue—a keeper.

- Rewrite all your keepers on a separate list.

- Now evaluate each keeper. Start with the finer points summarized below. e.g., Do you want to use a timeframe or not? Adjust as needed.

- Next: think about whether these are touchy questions or if you're nervous about asking them. If so, these are still keepers. You'll get tips for handling them in the next chapters.

- Finally, choose no more than four qualifying questions—the fewer, the better.

Summary of the finer points for qualifying

- Do you want to use a timeframe, or might it exclude too many prospects?

- Would your target market consider the question overly-aggressive or even rude?

- Is the question one you're essentially supposed to help answer?

- You want as few questions as possible: have you identified the bottom line?

- Whatever qualifying questions you end up with, be sure to adjust as new realities dictate.

What to do with the dumped questions

Most people end up with a lot of questions that do not belong in cold calls. Most of them belong in selling, so transfer them on over!

One more thing...

Some prospect groups, like IT managers, are famous for having zero patience with overviews, examples, benefit statements and so on. This means Format B is likely to annoy them right off the bat.

If Format B won't fly and you still want to qualify, identify the most important qualifier—just one—and fold it into Format A.

Example of qualifying in Format A:

WHY YOU'RE CALLING: We'd like to compete for IT projects you plan to outsource within the next few months.

ASK FOR NEXT STEP: Do you have any you're willing to discuss with me?

Remember: The above approach is reserved only for prospects who most likely will not appreciate Format B. Most do, so see the next chapters for using it to qualify.

Qualifying With Questions

Format B With Qualifying Questions

Who you are

Why you're calling

Ask permission

Give information (and transition)

Ask qualifying questions

Respond to answers

Ask for next step

Schedule

Prep, if desired

THIS APPROACH REDUCES problems because you give prospects information before you ask them to give information to you. You want to give as much or more information as you ask prospects to give you. Here are guidelines to help achieve the right balance:

- The information you give has to be meaningful. It won't work well if you rattle off verbiage just so you can get to the juicy questions.

- The best guideline is to write Give Info as if you will not ask any questions. To demonstrate this, some examples in this section pull from prior scripts.

Keeping the right balance includes using as few qualifying questions as possible. However, asking just one may be too few. I'll cover this in an example below.

You need to preface the qualifying questions with a reason—tell prospects why you're asking. Don't worry if you get stuck on this, you can use the approach where you qualify without asking direct questions. (It's covered in the next chapter.)

You also need to be ready to respond to what prospects tell you as they answer questions. The scripting for this will have to be general and you'll need two versions: one for qualified prospects, and one for non-qualified prospects.

The last thing to mention is that you may not want to include Prep, even though it's shown in the format. These calls take a bit longer and you've already imposed with some questions, asking more may be too much. Alright, now onto the examples!

Example #1

WHO YOU ARE: My name is Mary. I'm a commercial lines broker with Risk Management Consultants.

WHY YOU'RE CALLING: I'd like to briefly introduce my expertise and one of our programs. And then see where things may go from there.

ASK PERMISSION: Is this a good time?

GIVE INFORMATION: You may be aware there are a limited number of carriers with good programs for restaurants. We believe this highlights the importance of a broker's ability to act as consultant. We further believe we must have deep knowledge of clients' challenges to do that.

In order to provide expertise along with the right insurance, our brokers focus on certain industries. Restaurants is one of mine. My restaurant experience began in my parents' café and our kitchen table. Continued as I worked my way through college at large restaurants. Solidified over the past years as a broker.

I blend this experience with knowing each client as a unique entity. Because each has its risk management strengths and challenges. That's just an overview (T).

Our relationship with major carriers allows us to offer special programs. A few questions would highlight whether one may have value for your restaurant. Mind if I jump right in?

ASK QUALIFYING QUESTIONS: I think you have about (number) employees. Is that correct?

How many work 20 hours or more?

Do employees use their own vehicles to pick up supplies, make deliveries, or go to catered events?

RESPOND - QUALIFIED: Thank you. Sounds like one of our programs may provide excellent value. I'd like to explore this further.

ASK FOR NEXT STEP: Are you open to meeting soon to evaluate our services?

SCHEDULE: I'd like about one hour. What date and time work for you?

RESPOND - NOT QUALIFIED: Thank you. Based on the number of employees these programs would not necessarily provide added value. The differentiator would be more on the service side. I've got several colleagues who work with businesses of this size. Shall I have one of them call you?

Notes about the above example

The first thing I'd like to note is how this script explains why Mary wants to ask questions. She says, *"A few questions would highlight whether one may have value for your restaurant."*

Also notice Mary doesn't jump into those questions. She asks permission, which is quite effective.

This example has three questions to uncover baseline qualifiers for the special insurance program. There is certainly more to exploring a fit than that, and so Mary's response for qualified prospects still uses this strong consultative wording: *"may provide excellent value."*

Also notice the response for non-qualified prospects offers a referral to a colleague. This isn't always applicable so here is an example response that just bows-out:

"Thank you. Based on the number of employees the coverage you currently have is probably competitive. I appreciate the time you've given me. Shall we stay in touch?"

That kind of response continues to develop relationships and therefore possible referrals, and leaves the door open in case things change.

Last but not least: notice the response for non-qualified prospects is at the end of the script. You need both kinds of responses but don't put them next to each other. Qualified flows into asking for the next step, so that's what your script should do, too.

Format B example on next page...

Example #2

WHO YOU ARE: My name is Richard Sanderburg. I'm with ABC Marketing. My specialty is helping mid-size businesses make a big impression.

WHY YOU'RE CALLING: I'd like to give you a snapshot of our services and approach. Ask you a couple questions. And then see if we both think it makes sense to meet.

ASK PERMISSION: Do you have a few minutes?

GIVE INFORMATION: Let me start with the kinds of marketing we can handle. We can take care of everything from mail, to email, to interactive web marketing. We often handle branding for internal communiques. As well as newsletters. Clients tell us our approach is what sets us apart. Before we design and implement anything, we work on marketing strategy. That strategy includes how marketing will be maintained over time. Because that's how businesses get the most bang for their buck. That's the snapshot (T).

Of course, our services aren't necessarily a good fit for every organization. One high-level guideline is essentially based on buying in bulk.

ASK QUALIFYING QUESTIONS: Any major marketing projects in early planning stages at this time?

May I know if your marketing budget is $35,000 or more per year? That is just under $3,000 per month.

RESPOND - QUALIFIED: Thanks for sharing that information. It's certainly possible we may be an excellent partner. There would be a lot more we need to discuss.

ASK FOR NEXT STEP: Can we set up a meeting to do that?

SCHEDULE: Would you prefer to see me in person or talk things over on the phone?

RESPOND - NOT QUALIFIED: Thanks for sharing that information. Chances are low our particular skill set and resources would be a fit. I certainly appreciate your time here. Is there anything I might do for you?

Notes about the above example

Take a look at Why You're Calling and you'll see it mentions asking a "couple" questions. This means Richard won't need to ask permission to ask questions—he already did.

Richard really has only one qualifying question. But the question is based on dollars ($35,000) and so asking that one by itself would seem very selfish. Richard eases into the question by first asking about major projects. This may actually benefit him because some prospects may be beefing up their marketing for the first time.

The way Richard explains the reason for asking questions is *"Of course, our services aren't necessarily a good fit for every organization. One high-level guideline is essentially based on buying in bulk."* That analogy may work well with almost any prospect.

You may have noticed the responses for qualified and not-qualified prospects do not specifically mention the qualifying issues. This works because there are just a couple questions. If there were more than a couple questions the responses may need to be more specific (because the prospect was more specific, too). There are no concrete guidelines for this: experiment to see what works for you.

I'd also like to point out Richard asks non-qualified prospects, *"Is there anything I can do for you?"* Again, this gesture helps develop relationships, leaves doors open, and may generate some referrals.

How to Ask Extra-Tough Questions

THE WAY WE lead into qualifying questions makes a big difference, and explaining why we're asking these questions is a fundamental best practice.

There are several ways to lead into particularly nosy questions so we get pleasant answers. The examples below show one of each method.

Example: Do not ask for specifics

Let's use a script from our private banker, Rochelle. She is calling existing bank customers and can see their accounts.

This example shows just the qualifying parts. To get the full picture, imagine the example is tacked onto Rochelle's Format B script from an earlier chapter. She used a transition statement and then moves into qualifying.

PREFACE TO QUESTIONS: Like many bank services, ours have a baseline of certain account balances. I know these issues are personal and I don't expect specifics. But may I ask you some questions along those lines?

ASK QUALIFYING QUESTIONS: I can see the accounts you have here at Excalibur bank. Approximately how much do you keep with any other banks or credit unions?

May I know if any funds are reserved for purchasing property, kids' college, dream vacation or other things?

Last question, a salesy one. Do you think you may be open to moving some of your accounts?

Notes about the above example

Remember that prefacing questions with a reason why we're asking is a best practice. This isn't shown as a separate part of the script format, but I've shown it that way with the example.

To explain why she's asking the qualifying questions, Rochelle equates their services to everyday banking services. This is a practical way to position private banking requirements.

Rochelle also makes it clear she does not want specific dollar information. This makes the questions less invasive, and works with the reality that most of her prospects don't keep exact tabs on their balances.

There's a qualifying question about whether funds are likely to stay in accounts or not. The way it's worded also helps uncover potential fit for other private banking services, like mortgages or financial planning. This two-fer avoids asking too many qualifying questions.

Rochelle also asks prospects whether they'd be open to moving some accounts or not. She's learned the hard way some prospects aren't open to consolidating and so won't meet the minimums. She defuses the question's salesy nature by naming it that – "salesy."

Example: Ask gently

The prior example did not mention a specific dollar amount of $25,000 in accounts. Here's an example that asks about that directly yet gently. (Again, just showing the qualifying parts.)

PREFACE TO QUESTIONS: Like many bank services, ours have a baseline of certain account balances. Our clients maintain balances of at least $25,000.

ASK QUALIFYING QUESTIONS: I can see the accounts you have with us. May I know if your accounts would meet that baseline if outside accounts were included?

Thank you. And may I know if any funds are reserved for purchasing property, kids' college, dream vacation or other things?

Last question, a salesy one. Do you think you may be open to moving some of your accounts?

Notes about the above

Part of what makes the above example gentle is use of the phrase *"may I?"*

A bigger part of what makes it gentle—or not—is the caller's phone personality. Some people sound gentle, others may use the exact same wording but sound insincere or condescending. As you consider which approach will work well for you, consider what fits best with your personality (not what you think prospects will prefer). This brings us to the last method: humor.

Example: Use humor

The next example is from a consultant who helps business owners value and sell their businesses.

If this consultant looks for prospects who already know they want to sell their business, he won't find very many—it's too narrow a qualifier and the topic is very touchy. To keep things open and put the topic on the table at the same time, this caller uses Give Information to describe helping business owners decide if they may want to sell. A similar approach works well for other big decisions and changes, such as changing careers or retiring.

Below is what this consultant's script looks like as he transitions from Give Information into qualifying questions. Because this script works with delicate issues, the example includes responses for qualified and not qualified prospects.

TRANSITION AT END OF GIVE INFO: That's a couple examples of how I work with business owners.

Of course, my services aren't right for everyone. Timing also impacts whether it might make sense for us to talk further. So I'd like to ask some nosy questions about your savings habits, level of enthusiasm for working. Light topics. That okay with you?

ASK QUALIFYING QUESTIONS: In general, do you see your business as an asset you can convert to cash to augment personal savings?

On a scale of one to ten, one being the low. What's your level of enthusiasm for what you do at work, day-to-day?

Is there someone you plan to just hand the business to when you're ready to move on to something else?

RESPOND - QUALIFIED: Interesting. It's possible my services would provide good value because (caller describes this at a high level). We'd need to talk at length to determine that.

ASK FOR NEXT STEP: You interested in doing that?

RESPOND - NOT QUALIFIED: Thanks for your candor. Doesn't sound like my services would have value at this point but I'd like to get to know you better. How about a little networking. Can I buy you lunch?

Notes

Again, it's a caller's natural use of humor that makes the above effective (or not). Letting your personality come through makes your calls more powerful and attracts the right prospects. So if you're someone who uses humor, go for it. Otherwise, don't force it.

The explanation for why the caller wants to ask questions is, *"Timing also impacts whether it might make sense for us to talk further."* But you may have noticed the qualifying questions have nothing to do with timing. Here's why:

None of this caller's qualifying issues are cut and dried—not even timing. He chose questions that touch on hot buttons, which tend to prompt big responses...or not. It's the big responses that tell the caller the time is right and the prospect is qualified.

I'd also like to draw your attention to the response for qualified prospects. The note in parentheses means the caller extemporaneously talks about potential value or fit—he wings it a bit. If this will apply to your qualifying responses, use very general notes or a few bullet points in your script, otherwise you may sound a bit canned.

The last note for this example is about how "not qualified" asks prospects to do some networking. This is particularly appropriate for products and services that are often referred, like the above caller's services.

Qualifying Without Questions

Format B

Who you are

Why you're calling

Ask permission

Give information (and transition)

Ask for next step

Schedule

Prep, if desired

Not qualified

Semi-qualified

THIS IS THE same Format B covered several chapters ago. It can be used for qualifying by folding the issues into Give Information. Here's why this works so well:

- Prospects hear the qualifiers but have some personal distance from them. This makes the call much less invasive and so there's less push-back. This is one benefit of this approach.

- Many callers are very uncomfortable with asking direct qualifying questions. You don't have to do that with this approach. This is benefit number two.

- The qualifiers tend to jump out for prospects who do not meet them. Some will interject that they do not meet the qualifier, most will tell you that as they reply to your request for the next step. Either way, most will tell you if they're not qualified—you don't have to tell them. This is the third benefit of this approach.

The fourth benefit is greater ability to back-track on qualifiers if you want to. Here's the scoop...

When you ask direct qualifying questions, things seem more black and white to prospects. If they don't meet the qualifier but you ask to meet with them anyway, you may seem less professional or less sure of yourself.

In contrast, qualifiers seem less concrete when they're part of Give Info. And so when you say you'd still like to meet with prospects you seem flexible rather than unsure.

Potential downside

There will be some prospects who will not tell you they do not meet the qualifiers. They may have misunderstood, they may have been half-listening, or they may be yanking your chain. All in all, you may meet with more unqualified prospects.

Of course, direct qualifying questions have plenty of possible downside, too, including missing out on qualified prospects who were too annoyed to give you a chance.

TIP: Start With This Approach

Use the approach of folding qualifying into Give Info for a while. If you find you're meeting with too many unqualified prospects, switch to asking direct questions.

Now I'll show you some examples that fold qualifying into Give Info.

Example #1

The example is from Mary, the insurance broker. The qualifiers are: at least 30 employees, at least half working 20 or more hours, sometimes using their own vehicles. (Please note these are invented and so is the 'program.')

WHO YOU ARE: My name is Mary. I'm a commercial lines broker with Risk Management Consultants.

WHY YOU'RE CALLING: You may be aware there are a limited number of carriers with good programs for restaurants. I'd like to briefly introduce one of our special programs. And then see where things may go from there.

ASK PERMISSION: Do you have a couple minutes?

GIVE INFORMATION: Thank you. Our relationship with a major carrier allowed us to create a program designed for mid-size restaurants. Specifically. Restaurants with between 30 and 50 employees, half of them at 20 hours or more per week.

One feature of the program is its coverage for personal vehicle use. We know restaurants of this size often need someone to pick up supplies or make deliveries. They rarely want to send the owner or manager because they're focused on other things. Getting employees to catered events is yet another risk issue. This program covers such situations with extremely competitive premium cost. That is just one feature designed to benefit restaurants (T).

ASK FOR NEXT STEP: I'd like to see if this program, combined with our expertise, would be a good fit. Are you open to doing that?

NOT QUALIFIED: Thanks for letting me know. Shall we stay in touch? Things may change and we may have something that could be of interest.

SEMI-QUALIFIED: Thanks for letting me know. We have other programs that may provide value. Shall we set up a time to explore that?

Notes about the above

The first sentence in Why may look familiar because it used to be in Give Info. The idea behind including statements like that is they may spark more interest.

If you use something similar in your Why, do not make it a question like this: "Do you know few insurance carriers have good programs for restaurants?" Making it into a question makes it seem slightly rude or manipulative.

Notice how the qualifiers are part of Give Info but not the focus. This not only makes them more subtle, it gives the program's feature its rightful center stage.

Also note there is no separate scripting for qualified prospects, you'll just ask for the next step. However, there is scripting for not-qualified and semi-qualified. Most prospects will speak up and tell you if they don't meet the qualifiers but many will wait until you have asked for the next step. That's why these parts should be at the end of your script.

Need to be ready for semi-qualified?

At minimum, you will need to respond to prospects who are definitely not qualified. Many callers find they also need a version for prospects they still want to meet with, and that's what semi-qualified is for.

Example #2

The next example is from the marketing guy. Remember he has just one qualifier: a budget around $35,000.

When using direct questions, he added a question in front of that qualifier so he wouldn't look self-centered. He won't have to worry about that with this approach.

WHO YOU ARE: My name is Richard and I'm with ABC Marketing. My specialty is helping mid-size businesses make a big impression.

WHY YOU'RE CALLING: I'd like to give you a snapshot of our services. And then see if you think it makes sense to meet to explore a fit.

ASK PERMISSION: Do you have a couple minutes?

GIVE INFORMATION: Let me start with the kinds of marketing we can handle. We take care of everything from mail, to email, to interactive web marketing. We often handle internal communiques as well as newsletters.

Most clients have annual marketing budgets of $35,000 and up. And they tell us our process is what sets us apart. Before we design and implement anything, we work on strategy. That strategy includes how marketing will be maintained over time. Because that's how businesses get the most bang for their buck. That's the snapshot (T).

Of course, our services aren't necessarily a good fit for every company. I'd like to see if we'd be a good partner for yours.

ASK FOR NEXT STEP: Are you open to exploring the fit?

NOT-QUALIFIED: Thank you for letting me know. We're probably not the right marketing firm for you. Would you like some suggestions for other firms?

SEMI-QUALIFIED: We have clients who have similar situations and I'm game to discuss things if you are. What do you say?

Notes about the above example

If you say this example aloud I think you'll find the qualifier is still subtle. That's partly because (again) it's not the focus of Give Info. When you need to qualify prospects, don't let your own hot button be the focus because that will seem selfish and backfire.

You might also notice the qualifier begins the paragraph describing what clients say about the marketing firm's process. *"Most clients have annual marketing budgets of $35,000 and up."* At the end of that paragraph is this phrase: *"the most bang for their buck,"* which ties right back to the qualifier. Many callers are able to draw this kind of connection in their Give Info. However, simply stating the qualifier or qualifiers works just as well:

"Most clients have annual marketing budgets of $35,000 and up. And they tell us our process is what sets us apart. Before we design and implement anything, we work on strategy. That strategy includes how marketing will be maintained over time. Because that's part of marketing, too. That's the snapshot (T)."

The qualifier is very clear in both versions. Choose based on your own style and what fits most easily.

Next

That's the last example of qualifying without questions. Hopefully you can see how easy it is to fold qualifiers into Give Information instead of asking questions. However, there's one other option to consider: do not qualify at all.

Good Reasons to Skip Qualifying

TOO MANY PEOPLE include qualifying in their calls without first analyzing the true need for it. Their bosses say they have to, old sales dogs say they "should," or bad assumptive habits take over.

Unnecessary qualifying adds unnecessary effort and pulls results down. To help you avoid that, here's another way to look at the qualifying guideline for telemarketing:

Think about the prospects you plan to call. Imagine you reach them on the phone and right after you say who you are and why you're calling, they say your timing is amazing, they're looking for what you're selling and they want to meet as soon as possible.

Would you go for it? Or would you first need answers to two or three questions to help you decide?

If you'd go for it, you do not need to qualify and should leave it out of your calls.

More reasons to skip it

One reason to skip qualifying is when the practice with selling would do you good. Maybe you're new to selling. Maybe it's a new sales position or there are new services that involve a steep learning curve. Maybe your sales skills are rusty. If there's little risk you'd waste prospects' time, there would be no "wasted" sales meetings—just good practice.

Another good reason to skip qualifying is because you'd like to expand your network. Maybe you have a new business. Maybe it's a new territory or new prospect group or new sales position. Maybe you're just feeling isolated. Go meet with and get to know those people, qualified prospects or not!

Finally: skip qualifying if you need to swing the pendulum the other way. This often applies to people who have a lot of experience with cold calling—along with embedded counter-productive calling habits. Forcing yourself to leave qualifying completely out of calls usually clarifies any genuine need for it.

Let's take a break and look at scripts in context

Scripts/Calls In Context

WHEN WE MAKE calls, we say more than what's covered in the script formats. In particular, we ask to speak with a certain person or want to find out if the person who said "Hello?" is that person.

Some people try to cover that in their scripts, which is yet another thing that can make you sound canned. It also makes scripts cluttered, so they are less effective as guides.

However; when you have a good script, you already have all the wording you'll need for most situations. Let me show you what this sounds like...well, what it looks like, anyway.

You call a number. Someone answers, "Every Hair Salon. Can I help you?"

You know you're trying to reach Christina Aguilar so you say, *"May I speak with Christina Aguilar?"*

That someone asks, "Who is calling?"

You reply, *"My name is Devon. I have a cleaning company. I'd like to see if our services would be a good fit for the salon. Is Christina available?"*

Christina comes on the line and that's when you use your script, perhaps first throwing in, "Hi, Christina."

Here's another example:

You dial a residential number. Someone says, "Hello?"

You know you're trying to reach Jan Harris so you say, *"May I speak with Jan Harris?"*

The phone answerer says, "May I ask who's calling?"

You reply, *"My name is John. I'm a certified financial planner. I'd like to see if my services might be a good fit for Jan."* And then you wait.

Phone answerer then says, "I'm Jan."

You reply, "Great!" and head into your script, skipping the part where you say who you are.

You may have noticed that when the phone-answerers asked, "Who is calling?" the reply included who and why. That works well because—as a stranger—who you are is mostly about the reason for your call.

One more thing…

I want to point out the examples that use *"May I speak with…"* That is very different from starting with "Is this Christina Aguilar?"

The latter can be particularly invasive because an unidentified stranger is asking, so here's one more example of context:

You make a call. Someone answers, "Every Hair Salon. Can I help you?"

You say, *"Yes. My name is Devon. I have a cleaning company and I'd like to see if our services would be a good fit for the salon. I think I'm looking for Christina Aguilar. Is this Christina?"*

Next

We just covered a bit of what to say and do after a human answers your call. What a perfect segue to Gatekeeper script formats and calls!

GATEKEEPER CALLS

Don't Mess with Gatekeepers

When You Need Help Reaching Someone

When You're Not Sure of the Contact

More Examples & Tips

When Gatekeepers Say No

Don't let what you cannot do interfere with what you can do.

(John Wooden)

Don't Mess With Gatekeepers

THE GATEKEEPER CONCEPT is based on the idea these people can open the phone-gate and connect you to your prospects...or keep you out.

A gatekeeper is anyone who answers the phone but is not your known prospect or contact. This includes receptionists, operators, administrative assistants, bosses and coworkers.

Most of the time these folks ask callers some version of "What is the call about?"

Many callers answer with attempts at subterfuge. They say it's a personal matter or they're following up on something, among other fibs. Some callers flatly lie and say they're returning the prospect's call or that the call is expected, tossing an authoritative tone in with the lie. All of that happens because these callers think it will prevent those rascal phone-answerers from "blocking" their call.

There are 823 reasons why hiding or avoiding the truth won't work well. Here are just four:

- The phone-answerer may be able to help you, or they may be the person you actually want to talk with. Starting with BS will not make a good impression.

- Many phone-answerers will recognize the disingenuous attempt and block it all the more. After all, they can play games, too.

- Many prospects will not be pleased if you treat their coworker or assistant with a lack of respect. Making it harder for people to do their job—which includes finding out what the call is about—falls into this category.

- Avoiding the truth is inconsistent with a consultative approach. Fibbing to gatekeepers and then switching to another approach with prospects takes more energy and effort (with little or no pay off).

So don't try to get around gatekeepers, treat them with the same respect you treat prospects. You may be amazed at how well this works.

What's in this section

Once we let go of trying to "get past" gatekeepers things are pretty straightforward, so I won't beat up any scripts. Instead, I'll show you good examples along with tips. Let's start by revisiting a basic situation that doesn't need an additional format.

"Who is calling?"

If you answer the above question with just your name and company, here's what usually happens next: gatekeeper puts you on hold, tells the prospect your name, prospect tells gatekeeper she doesn't know you, and gatekeeper comes back on the line and says something like, "She's not available." End of call.

This happens because when you're a stranger (yes, you're a stranger) who you are is mostly about why you're calling.

The good news is you have all the words you need to prevent such problems in your Contact/Prospect script. When asked who you are, reply with Who and Why.

For example, the gatekeeper asks, "Who is calling?" and you reply: *"My name is Steve. I'm with a company that provides technology support. I'd like to see if our services might be a good fit for your company."* And then stop talking. Give the gatekeeper a chance to respond.

Warnings for after Who and Why

After you've said Who and Why, you may want to add, "Is Prospect in?" However, be careful with this.

Do not use that as some sort of technique to make gatekeepers put you through (it won't work very well). Pay attention to your tone, as well. An imperious tone will irk many gatekeepers.

Also avoid adding statements like, "Can you put me through?" These tend to be heard as condescending or demanding whether you mean it that way or not.

Your best bet is to be silent after saying Who and Why.

Be brave and be silent

As we remain silent, there's usually silence on the other end of the line as the gatekeeper decides what to do next. That pause can make us nervous, and we sometimes talk too much when we're nervous. We start explaining why our products are great, talk about where we met the prospect, say that we sent them a letter, and so on. All of this backfires because it irritates gatekeepers.

If you met the prospect, include that upfront in Who and Why. *"My name is Steve. I'm with Computer Crossing. Met Joyce at the chamber mixer last week. I'd like to see if our services might be a good fit for your company."*

Otherwise, be quiet after you say Who and Why. If needed, count silently to ten.

You may want to be proactive

Instead of waiting to see if you are asked about your call, you may want to proactively say Who and Why. This can be particularly effective when calling consumers at home. For example:

Person answers phone and says, "Hello?"

You say, *"My name is Sean and I'm with ABC Bank. We're new to the area. I'd like to see if Prospect might be interested in our services. Is Prospect home?"*

Next

Now onto the gatekeeper script formats.

One format gets you help when you've left a ton of messages and need to try something else.

The other format is used when you're not sure who you should ask for (you don't have a contact name).

Both formats prevent you from being your own worst enemy by making gatekeepers mad.

Need Help Reaching A Prospect?

GATEKEEPERS CAN BE very helpful when we're having trouble getting in contact with someone. The format is simple:

- Who you are

- Why you're calling the person (the prospect)

- Ask for help

Example #1

WHO YOU ARE: My name is Sydney. I'm with ABC Bank.

WHY YOU'RE CALLING THE PERSON: We'd like the chance to earn the company's business. I've been trying to reach James to talk about this, with no luck.

ASK FOR HELP: Can you help me with something? Would you suggest a good time to reach him?

Example #2

WHO YOU ARE: My name is Sydney. I'm with ABC Bank.

ASK FOR HELP: Can you help me with something?

WHY YOU'RE CALLING THE PERSON: We'd like the chance to earn your company's banking business. I've been trying to reach James to talk about this, with no luck. Can you suggest a better time or way to reach James?

Notes about the above examples

These examples use very similar words but flip format order around a bit. Either order works well.

Both examples include a rhetorical, *"Can you help me with something?"* AND a specific request. Using both tends to get better results than just one or the other. It's particularly useful to ask for help because that's the best way to receive it.

Notice the second example asks if there is a better way to reach the prospect; as in other than the phone. Many gatekeepers know if our prospects prefer email or mail (or phone). When treated with respect, they'll often share that valuable information.

Gatekeepers will also often help us with information about bad days or times to reach prospects. For example: the days when a prospect prepares for and then runs a weekly meeting, times when a prospect leaves the office because she's got a very long commute, and so on.

Not Sure Who to Contact?

THOUGH THE INTERNET makes it easier to build our own lists, there are still plenty of reasons to get information from humans in the prospect-companies. The second gatekeeper script format is perfect for this:

- Who you are
- Why you're calling the company
- Ask for help
- (Likely contacts, if needed)

Example #1

WHO YOU ARE: My name is Brian. I work with executives and their direct teams to improve planning and communication.

WHY CALLING THE COMPANY: I'd like to see if my services may be of use in your organization.

ASK FOR HELP: Can you direct me a bit? Would you suggest who I might talk with about that?

(LIKELY CONTACTS) May be a senior person in your training group. Perhaps the head of HR.

Example #2

WHO YOU ARE: This is Samuel calling. My company helps take a lot of the hassle out of printing things like reports, presentations and training materials.

WHY CALLING THE COMPANY: I'd like the chance to earn your company's business.

ASK FOR HELP: Would you suggest who I should contact? Would it be you?

(LIKELY CONTACTS): Could be someone in marketing, training, or both.

Why this works so well

The best way to explain why these scripts work so well is to contrast them with another approach. Take Samuel, the printing guy. He could call and ask, "Who manages the printing for your company?" There are two problems with that approach, starting with a big one: it's the kind of call most gatekeepers shut right down.

In addition, there may not be a person who "manages" printing. Since that's all Samuel said—he didn't ask for help—most gatekeepers will respond with vague objections designed to get him off the phone. Treating gatekeepers professionally and politely, including stating the core reason for our call, is a much more effective approach.

That goes double when it turns out the gatekeeper is our prospect. This is a common situation when calling smaller companies because employees wear more hats and anyone may answer the phone. That's why Samuel's script includes *"Would it be you?"*

TIP: Have titles or roles ready

I'd like to draw your attention to the "(Likely Contacts, if needed)" part of these scripts. It's in parentheses because you only use it if the gatekeeper is drawing a blank.

Before you call: determine probable work titles, job roles, or departments for your prospects. Include these in your scripts so you're ready to offer them if the gatekeeper seems to need more information or direction.

More Gatekeeper Scripts and Tips

HERE ARE A few more example gatekeeper scripts for certain scenarios.

When you need more time to describe what you do

(Ask and use permission)

WHO YOU ARE: My name is Brian.

ASK FOR HELP: I need some help figuring out who I should ask for. Can I tell you what I do and get suggestions?

WHY CALLING THE COMPANY: I work with senior executives and their teams. This includes helping with planning sessions. And improving communication with each other and with employees. I'd like to see if these services would be of interest. Would you suggest who I should talk with about that?

Note

Do not proceed with the Why unless you get permission. When gatekeepers say they are busy or will not be able to help you—or any other form of "no"—say thanks and move on to the next call.

When you need to confirm or update information

WHO YOU ARE: My name is Mary. I'm a commercial insurance broker.

WHY CALLING PERSON OR COMPANY: I'd like to send your CFO something and I'm not sure I have the right contact information.

ASK FOR HELP: Can you confirm or correct what I have?

Note

This may not work well if your information is completely off because it can seem like a sly end-run. If your list is way out of date, start fresh and use the format for finding who you should contact.

When you're looking for a new contact

Below is an example of calling when the known contact/prospect is not responding and you want to see if there are others in the department or group. I've shown "Prospect" to indicate the person's actual name but you should not do that in your scripts. Leave a blank or something that won't lure you into using the wrong name.

WHO YOU ARE: My name is Samuel and I work for a printing company.

ASK FOR HELP: Can you help me with something?

WHY CALLING COMPANY: I'd like to see if our services might come in handy. I've been trying to reach Prospect with no luck. Would you suggest someone who works with Prospect? An admin or training coordinator maybe?

Notes

You might have noticed the example script asks for someone "below" the prospect. This implements a strategy to find and connect with people who use your products or services more directly. They often influence, screen, and even control purchases, which can make them great contacts.

You'll need to determine likely titles or roles for these prospects so you can fold it into your call. Do that proactively this time, don't wait to see if the gatekeeper draws a blank.

Calling the gatekeeper more than once

The situation for the above example often means you're calling the same number or gatekeeper again, but with a different request this time.

Because gatekeepers often remember your first call, be ready to explain why you're asking for someone else. For example, *"I often work directly with coordinators and assistants. So I'd like to connect with them, too."*

As for going "up" the ladder, it may be better to research these contacts on the web and then call. It's hard to succeed with calls that ask, "Can you tell me who Prospect's boss is?"

"Is this a sales call?"

Tell the truth! The answer is either *"yes"* or *"In a way, it's a prospecting call."*

When Gatekeepers Say "No"

IT'S ACTUALLY RARE for gatekeepers to simply say they will not help us. They're more likely to tell us there is no better time or way to reach the prospect, they don't have information, or they are not allowed to give out information.

I assure you those things are usually true. But it doesn't matter whether the gatekeeper is telling the truth or not. If we try to figure that out, we can get sucked right into game-playing and we will lose. So don't go there even in your mind. Just thank them and try other things (see below).

"He's not interested"

It is quite common for gatekeepers to tell us our prospect will not be interested, or there is no need, or they already have what we're offering. In these cases, use a matter-of-fact or light tone (avoid sounding dismissive) and try responses like these:

"Thanks for letting me know. I'd like to try to connect anyway."

"Fair enough. Well, I'd like to leave a voicemail. Can you put me through?"

When calling small businesses (in which gatekeepers often play a larger role) it may be more effective to handle the "no" as an objection. Same applies when calling consumers at home. See the handling objections section for tips.

More tips

The old technique of calling before and after normal work hours still works very well. We often need prospects' direct lines for this, but it's worth a shot even when we don't.

However, do not use that tactic soon after the gatekeeper tells you the prospect specifically said she was not interested. Doing so would seem disrespectful.

Ah, but what if you think the gatekeeper just said something to blow you off? Playing games wastes your time and energy. Let it go.

I also want to remind you there are other marketing tools to use. When having trouble reaching prospects by phone, try using other tools.

NAP?

Someone you cannot reach is not a prospect. That's true if they're not picking up, if they're not calling back, or if the gatekeeper won't help you. Put calling this prospect aside for a few months and then try again.

A repeat mini-lecture

Callers who have had gatekeeper-type jobs (including yours truly) do not have trouble with gatekeepers! They instinctively treat gatekeepers with respect. They also know anyone answering the phone may wield influence, may have useful information, or may be the person they most want to talk with. Treat all gatekeepers as if they are your prospect and you, too, will reap the rewards.

Key Points, and Next

Treat "gatekeepers" the same way you treat known prospects. Be direct and upfront about the reason for your call—including that you would like their help—and use consultative wording about the potential fit.

If the gatekeeper won't let you talk with the contact/prospect, that's the same as not being able to reach that contact/prospect. Don't let NAPs look like a delicious challenge—use other marketing tools, try again way down the road, or let go.

At this point in the book, we've covered contact/prospect scripts, qualifying, and gatekeeper scripts. We've also covered how to use Give Information to help prevent objections. Alas, we cannot prevent all objections (gosh darn those humans), so it's time to cover how to handle them.

HANDLING OBJECTIONS

Train Your Brain

How to Handle Objections Like:

"No Thanks"

"All Set"

"I'm Happy"

"We Do That Ourselves"

And More

If there is no wind, row.

(Latin proverb)

Train Your Brain

LET'S REVIEW IMPORTANT fundamentals before we get into the fine art of handling objections.

Embrace reality: luck is a factor, and we cannot make people do stuff.

Remember there are things we can do to put luck on our side and keep doors open. Many of the preceding pages covered ways to do that, and this section will add more.

Remember you're marketing or prospecting, not selling. Applying sales techniques for handling objections will definitely backfire. You need a different approach—which you're about to get—as well as a different mindset.

How a positive trait bites back

People who use telemarketing tend to be in roles which include problem-solving. Most have an aptitude for dealing with challenges and are often highly attracted to them. These are valuable traits when selling, but they tend to bite you when prospecting, especially when it comes to handling objections. Here's how:

Prospects say they don't have time? Let's ignore that and tell them how a mere 20 minutes will be worth dropping everything else. Prospects say they're not interested? Let's tell them why they should be. Prospects say they're happy with their current provider? Let's tell them why we would be so much better.

In other words...let's act as if our call should be their priority, lecture them, and tell them their first choice was wrong. While we're at it, let's waste our own time, effort and energy, too.

You can see why that approach doesn't work well. There are far more successful methods and they're all grounded in this mindset: your objective is to look for and focus on opportunities. Let the big, juicy challenges go.

What's an "opportunity"?

Because many CRM use the term "opportunity," I need to warn you about using related built-in features. Most CRM's "opportunity" applies to early selling and will steer you wrong when prospecting.

The solution is to ignore the CRM—and its related built-in features—and use a human-based definition suitable for the realities of telemarketing. When telemarketing, you're looking for these things, in this order:

- You're looking for people who are willing to hear what you have to say.

- Qualifying aside, you're next looking for people who are open to exploring the business fit (often in a separate sales conversation).

Key concepts for handling objections

As mentioned once or twice before, luck is a factor we must embrace. This key concept applies to handling objections, too. If people are open to another viewpoint, great. If they're not, don't push it.

The second key concept: True opportunities are based on a prospect's willingness and openness, not on our use of techniques to change their mind. Forcing things rarely sticks once we've hung up the phone.

The third key concept: You need something to work with...but most objections are vague.

The reality of vague objections

Think about the objections you most often hear when calling. These probably include versions of:

"I'm good."

"No thanks."

"We're all set."

"Not at this time."

"Not interested."

These comments are clearly objections—but about what? In a sales situation, we'd apply various techniques to find out, but when cold calling these techniques only make things worse.

If we make a supposedly educated guess, we're being assumptive. If we push the prospect to say more and they comply, we invariably argue the point, which seems disrespectful. Neither of those get us very far and if we persist most doors close even tighter.

As we try to dig into the prospect's vague statement, we're also wasting our own time and energy. By working extra-hard on these challenges, we have much less energy and time for actual opportunities.

So don't try to push the river

Prospects who have vague objections are not hiding something, they're not willing to hear us out and/or not open to exploring the fit. Trying to change this is like trying to push a river.

Instead of arguing, instead of making assumptions, instead of annoying prospects and wasting your time: put luck on your side using the call-back strategy.

The Call-Back Strategy

THE CENTRAL IDEA of prospecting is to give ourselves lots of opportunities to reach the right people at the right time. Fortunately, this is not a now-or-never situation. When we've called at the 'wrong' time, we put luck on our side by trying again and again. The call-back strategy ensures you apply that best practice. The strategy is very effective and very simple.

A common situation

Let's start by painting a common picture. You've said what you want to say and the prospect replied, "No thanks." To put luck on your side, you're going to call again.

The old tactic is to tell the prospect you plan to call back and when you will do that e.g., "I'll follow up in a couple months." This does not work well because you're acting as if you assume they'll be interested later and that you're the best judge of their timing (which most prospects find annoying).

Another tactic is to call again without telling the prospect that's what you plan to do. This actually works fine and you should feel free to apply this approach. When using this approach, it's not necessary—or helpful—to tell prospects you plan to call again. Just wrap up the call with something like, "*Okay. Have a good day,*" hang up, and move on.

What works even better is to <u>ask</u> if you can call again, which is the heart of the call-back strategy.

Call-back strategy in full

Here is the entire strategy. Notice two of the steps are optional!

Step 1: Ask if you can call back down the road.

Optional Step 2: If the prospect says you may: ask for a general time frame to call again.

Optional Step 3: If the time frame sounds somewhat specific, see if there's a reason behind that.

Now I'll walk through each step.

Step 1 works well all by itself

The first step is to ask if you can call again. This demonstrates respect for prospects and therefore helps build relationships with them. Examples what to say for this step:

"Mind if I call you back?"

"Can I check in with you down the road?"

"Okay if I try you again sometime?"

When prospects give you the okay to call back: say thanks, hang up, and set a reminder to call again using whatever timing you wish. As long as you follow through and call again, you're putting luck on your side.

The highly effective call-back strategy is as simple as that. You can add even more power to it by applying Step 2, but first I should cover how to handle "no."

When the prospect says "no"

Back to our picture: you said what you wanted to say and the objection from the prospect was, "No, thanks. We're all set."

You ask, *"Can I check back down the road?"*

The prospect again says, "No, thanks."

Well, drat. What now? You've got two excellent options.

One option is to let go completely: don't call, don't write, don't email—do not pop the prospect back into the top of the funnel at all.

The other option is to call again much later; e.g., four months or more in the future. When you make the next call, do not mention your first call and don't worry if the wording is exactly the same, just make the call. (Most prospects will not remember the prior call, and very few will remember it in detail.)

If they say 'no' again, repeat the above. This is how you put luck on your side!

Re-busting the six calls myth

Remember that the idea you need to call a prospect six or eight or whatever times before they move forward has no basis in reality. Don't let this myth stick a number of calls in your head. I'll tell you how to set and apply a realistic number in a later chapter.

Step 2 is optional

Back to our picture again: You said what you wanted to say and the objection from the prospect was, "No, thanks. I'm all set."

You asked, *"Can I check back down the road?"*

The prospect said, "Sure."

If you want to go a bit further; take optional Step 2 and invite the prospect to suggest <u>when</u> you would try again. Here are three examples of what this sounds like:

"Don't want to pester you. Would you suggest a general timeframe for me to check back?"

"Can you give me a rough timeline for another try, so I don't impose?"

"Would you suggest a general timeline for me to give you another call?"

This continues to show respect for their time. This also develops relationships a bit more because now you've had a tiny conversation.

This approach has one more bonus: your guess for timing is never as good as the prospect's. Using their guideline actually makes it easier to manage your own time and effort. Ultimately, it's also more effective.

Very important tips about Step 2

Stopping after Step 1 works quite well. Step 2 is truly optional.

When you do take Step 2, you are <u>not</u> asking for an appointment or a specific date or time. Make sure this is clear in your mind, tone of voice, and words you use; otherwise, it will backfire.

Many people need to practice Step 2 so the premise sinks in and they have an appropriately light tone. You, too, may want to practice ahead of using it.

This next tip may seem repetitive but it's necessary: you are not asking for an appointment and when prospects give you a timeframe that does not mean they have agreed to explore the fit. You are still marketing (not selling).

The above is true even when prospects give you a specific or somewhat specific timeline. They are not indicating an interest in having a sales conversation, they're just answering your polite question.

That said, when a prospect mentions a somewhat specific timeframe you may want to see if there's a reason behind it.

Sounds specific? Optional step 3

Here we go: you said what you wanted to say and the objection from the prospect was, "No, thanks. I'm all set."

You asked, *"Can I check back down the road?"*

The prospect said, "Sure."

You lightly said, *"I don't want to pester you. Would you suggest a general timeframe for me to check back?"*

Most prospects will tell you to call back in a couple or few months, six months, next quarter or next year. These are common and general responses.

However, some prospects will use timeframes that sound more specific; e.g., two and a half months, six weeks, or five months. You may want to see if there's a reason behind such timeframes because this may uncover useful information. This is what optional Step 3 is for.

Let's say the prospect replied, "Give it about ten weeks."

Step 3: Acknowledge what the prospect said and then casually ask if there's a reason behind it. For example:

"Great. I'll give you a call in about ten weeks. I have to say I'm a little curious. Is there anything going on between now and ten weeks?"

There may or may not be a reason

Just because a timeframe sounds specific, that doesn't mean there's a reason behind it. Many prospects will simply answer, "No, no particular reason." On the other hand, some prospects will have a reason and will tell you things like:

"I'm getting married and then going on a honeymoon."

You should congratulate them, of course. You should also ask about these events when you call again.

"I just got promoted and will be looking for new vendors."

Hooray! But you should still treat the next call as a prospecting call.

Prospects may also say something like:

"It's tax season and I'm swamped now."

You may feel embarrassed you didn't know that. Don't let this get you down—you know it now!

"I've heard the company is up for sale."

This could affect prospecting in positive or negative ways. Keep an eye out for news and go from there.

"I'm giving notice and the new person should be in place by then."

Wish them the best of luck. Do not ask who that new person will be. If applicable: go ahead and ask if you can contact them at their new place of work. (Be sure to give them plenty of time to get settled before you call.)

Tips for Step 3

You can stop after Step 1 and that will help put luck on your side. You can stop after Step 2 and that will help put luck on your side. Using Step 3 is optional.

If you use Step 3 in response to almost every timeframe this becomes a hollow technique—which will backfire—so use it sparingly. Use Step 3 only when the prospect gave you a timeframe that sounds more specific than you usually hear.

People who haven't made many calls sometimes have trouble differentiating common timeframes from more specific (less common) timeframes. For this reason, it may be better add Step 3 after you've had some experience.

Call-back strategy examples

Using Step 1 only:

Prospect says, "Not right now."

You say, *"Okay. Mind if I call again sometime?"*

Prospect says that's fine. You say, *"Will do. Have a great day."* And hang up.

Using Step 1 and Step 2 only:

Prospect says, "Not right now."

You ask, *"Okay if I try again at some point?"*

Prospect says that's fine.

With a little humor in your voice you say, *"Thanks. I don't want to be a total pest. Would you suggest a general timeframe for me to try back?"*

Prospect tells you, "Give it two or three months."

You say, *"Will do. Until then."* You hang up, make a reminder note, and go on to the next call.

Using Step 1, Step 2 and Step 3 (because the prospect uses a specific-sounding timeframe):

Prospect says, "Not right now."

You ask, *"Okay if I try again down the road?"*

Prospect says that's fine.

You say, *"I'm sure you're busy. Would you suggest a general timeline for me to call again?"*

Prospect tells you, "After the 12th of August."

You say, *"I'll make a note of that."* After a short pause you casually add, *"I'm intrigued, is there something happening on August 12?"*

Prospect says he's applied for his ex-boss's job. He'll either be looking for new providers (like you) or looking for a new employer. You wish him the best of luck, hang up, make a reminder note, and move on to the next call.

One more example using Steps 1, 2 and 3:

Prospect says, "Not right now."

You ask, *"Okay if I try again down the road?"*

Prospect says that's fine.

You say, *"I'm sure you're busy. Would you suggest a general timeline for me to call again?"*

Prospect tells you, "After the end of September."

You casually say, *"I'll make a note of that. I'm a little curious, is there something happening when September ends?"*

Prospect tells you that's when he finishes tax returns for clients who filed an extension.

You: *"Oh, of course. Thanks for the reminder. Have a great day."* You hang up, make a reminder note, and remove other tax pros from your call list for now.

Key Points, and What's Next

We want to give ourselves lots of opportunities to reach the right people at the right time. This is not a now-or-never situation, nor is it blind luck. Instead, we put luck on our side by calling prospects more than once. This has been the case from the beginning of telemarketing, and is still the case. The call-back strategy puts best practices to work with added power.

The call-back strategy works extremely well for vague objections; such as, "We're all set" and "Not interested." In fact, using other methods usually annoys prospects and wastes our time and energy.

The call-back strategy also works well for more specific objections, such as, "We do that in-house." However, there are additional methods which are often more effective with these objections and I'll cover those next.

Handling Specific Objections

THE CENTRAL IDEA and realities of prospecting apply whether dealing with vague or specific objections. Luck is a factor. The way we put luck on our side is to call more than once and the call-back strategy helps ensure we apply this best practice. It's the only effective method for handling vague objections, but we have additional options for objections that are more specific.

Handling common stumpers

I'll start with objections that tend to stump us. They're not exactly vague, but prospects aren't necessarily saying what they mean, either (gosh darn those humans). Here are tips for handling these.

"I'll call you"

Common versions of this objection include:

"What's the website? I'll call you if I'm interested."

"I'll get back to you."

The best way to respond is to ask permission to call if you don't hear from them. For example, *"Fair enough. Do you mind if I touch base if I don't hear from you?"*

In other words, use Step 1 of the call-back strategy.

If the prospect says that's okay, use Step 2, e.g., *"Thanks. I don't want to be a pest. Would you suggest a general timeframe I could use?"*

Leave it at that: do not add Step 3.

What if the prospect does not say you may call them?

Let it go, dear caller (e.g., *"Okay. Thanks again for your time"*). Someone who won't talk with you is not a good challenge, they are NAP: Not a Prospect.

Timing is off

Sometimes timing—also known as luck—is just off. This is the case when you hear things like:

"I'm too busy."

"We're not looking to make any changes."

Prospects who say things like that are telling you why they are not open to talking. If you try to "overcome" this, you only signal a lack of respect, so use the call-back strategy instead (all three steps, if you wish).

Timing and luck are also off when prospects tell you they've recently made a change with statements like:

"We just entered a new contract."

"We're implementing a new system."

"We've only been using this program for a few months."

When a change was just made, prospects are rarely open to considering alternatives. The call-back strategy works well in this situation; however, you may want to position things a bit differently. For example:

"Thanks for letting me know. It's important to give new systems time, of course. Would you mind if I checked in at some point?"

If they agree, use Step 2. *"Thanks. What would be a reasonable timeframe?"* (Do not use Step 3.)

TIP: Notice the above was not, "...give new systems time, of course. <u>But</u> would you mind if I checked in at some point?" Leaving out the word "but" ensures you don't accidentally slam something they just purchased.

"Send me something"

This objection has driven callers crazy since way back when the only thing we could send was a brochure. Even then, we tried to engage prospects by explaining we had more than one brochure available (which was often a fib) so we could ask what kind of information would interest them.

These days, callers often try to engage prospects by alluding to a vast library of articles, white papers, case studies, and videos—asking the prospect to pick something. After the prospect makes a selection, we gather some information (now added to CRM instead of scribbled on a paper list) and then ask when we should follow up.

The truth is, both parties know the brief interaction is a bit of a farce (which was also true way back when). So instead of taking the "send me something" statement and running with it, try this:

With good humor in your head, heart and tone of voice, *"Oh, no, not the dreaded send me something! Be happy to. But is this a polite thanks but no thanks?"*

This tends to lighten the mood at the same time it clarifies things.

For prospects who really are saying no thanks: do not send them anything, use the call-back strategy. For example, *"No problem, I get it. Is it okay if I give you another try down the road?"*

Here are tips for prospects who actually <u>do</u> want you to send something:

- Do not consider available options as tools to get into the prospect's head because that's putting way too much into this exchange. Just offer the options and send the one they want.

- If you are sending via email, be sure to ask if you may add them to your email list in general; otherwise, it's not a true opt-in.

- Do not use an assumptive follow-through, use the same wording in the call-back strategy. For example, *"I'd like to check in. Would you suggest a general timeframe for me to give you a call?"*

All of the above reinforces a respectful approach, which helps build relationships.

When you follow through and make that next call: ask if they had a chance to read or watch what you sent, but do not make that the focus of your call. (I'll provide tips on this a bit later.)

Now let's turn to the other common and specific objections.

Common specific objections

The prior chapter opened with explaining many objections we hear are vague and don't give us anything to work with. So what's a specific objection? Here are examples:

"I've got a broker."

"We've been with our bank for ten years."

"We handle that in-house."

"My research assistant does that."

"I do that myself."

"We have an excellent rate."

"We don't need a new..."

"I already have a..."

All of those objections—and many more—are really versions of "I'm happy."

Common errors with specific objections

We're often taught to handle objections by offering a counter-position. This means the prospect says they are happy and we counter by saying they should not be, which tends to backfire.

When we try to handle these objections by suggesting our products or services would probably be better, we're also saying their current provider—one they may have personally selected—is not as good. As you might imagine, this doesn't go over well.

If we try to handle this type of objection by saying the prospect's peers prefer what we offer, we're also saying we assume the prospect has the same wants and needs. This doesn't work well because most people want to be treated as having unique wants and needs.

Last but not least, we are a stranger to the prospect and therefore have little to no credibility. Our assertions rarely make them rethink their happiness, it just makes them think up ways to get us off the phone.

How to counter happiness

Imagine the prospect says a version of, "We're happy." Without being assumptive and without arguing with that happiness, is there a reason they may want to talk with you, anyway? Yup! There are three reasons they may want to talk with you:

Compare

They may want to compare what you offer to what they currently have. This is different from saying they *should* compare. It's also different from saying they may want to compare because your product/service is or may be better.

Complement

They may want to see if what you offer complements—works with—what they have. This is different from saying your product/service fills gaps (which would suggest there are gaps). Nor are you saying their current situation needs improvement.

Just in case

They may want to have more information so they know their options, just in case.

Just in case what? In case their needs change, in case their current what or whomever stops doing a good job or raises rates too much or goes out of business...

However, you're not saying these things will happen—you're not even mentioning the possibilities. You're only saying it may be good to have known options, just in case.

Their perspective, your mindset

Notice all of the above reasons use the word "may." This consultative word signals the reality that it's the prospect who decides whether she wants to talk more with you.

Sure, you're making a suggestion, but it's up to them to accept it or not. As you make these suggestions, remember your goal is to work with opportunities, not to overcome every single objection.

It's also important to know these suggestions are not sneaky ways to get your foot in the door. When prospects accept the suggestion, it will be important to honor the nature of the agreement. I'll cover this issue in a bit, for now, let's look at examples.

How to counter with "compare"

I'll give you several examples and then explain the finer points.

Prospect says, "We're happy with our current..."

You say, *"That's true for most business owners I talk with and many decide to sit down with me so they can do a comparison. How does that sound to you?"*

Prospect says, "I handle my own..."

You reply, *"I hear that often, and many people choose to meet so they can do a comparison. How about meeting with me on that basis?"*

Prospect says, "We already take credit cards."

You say, *"There are lots of good options out there, that's for sure. And many business owners meet with me to do a quick comparison. Does that interest you?"*

Prospect says, "We've been with our bank for ten years."

You reply, *"I've been hearing that a lot, lately. And a number of CFOs decided to meet with me because it had been a while since they ran a comparison. Would you like to do the same?"*

Tips & finer points

Notice the examples talk about people other than the prospect. The caller mentions "business owners," "CFOs" and "people," but does not even add "like you."

That wording gives prospects some space. Since you're not backing prospects into a verbal corner, they're less likely to push back. Talking about other people also acknowledges the objection without giving it more power—shows you're not afraid of it.

Notice use of the word "and." It sits between acknowledging the objection, and the counter to that objection. Here's what that looks like if we use the word "but" in its place: "I hear that often, but many people choose to meet so they can do a comparison."

The word "but" discounts the first statement, essentially saying the prospect's objection has little merit. Telling prospects they're wrong doesn't work very well.

In contrast, the word "and" creates a smooth bridge from the issue to the counter. In this case, a smooth bridge from the objection to the idea of comparing. The message is that the objection and counter have equal merit, which brings me to the next tip: be sure to find out if the prospect accepts the counter.

Notice the above examples end with a direct question to the prospect, e.g.: *"How does that sound to you?"* or *"How about meeting with me on that basis?"* These questions check in with the prospect to see if they accept the counter and are willing to move forward.

Using a clear question (instead of assuming they accept) demonstrates respect for the prospect. Using a clear question also helps you get a clear yes or no—so you know if you are still marketing or moving into selling.

Include a reason to compare?

The above objection-counters purposely do not include a reason to compare—there's no mention of comparing to see if we can save prospects money, time, etc.

One purpose behind this omission is to avoid sounding assumptive or dismissive. For example: if we say, "compare to see if our rates would be lower," many prospects think we're saying they're paying too much. As noted, this tends to close more doors than it opens.

Another purpose is to keep the possible reasons wide open. There are many reasons why a prospect may want to compare and we cannot predict which reason will appeal to which prospect.

On the other hand, some callers find it's effective to mention a reason for comparison. Here are a couple examples to help you choose what's best for your target market:

Prospect says, "We've been with our bank for ten years."

You reply, *"I've been hearing that a lot, lately. And a number of CFOs decided to meet with me because it had been a while since they compared services, rates, and so on. How does that sound to you?"*

Prospect says, "We handle printing in-house."

You counter with, *"Several clients handled their printing in-house and decided to do a comparison to our services. See how convenience, cost and quality shakes out. How about meeting with me to do the same?"*

Or you may have replied, *"Many companies handle their printing in-house and like to do a comparison to our services. See how convenience, cost and quality shakes out. How about meeting with me to do the same?"* Note this refers to "companies" instead of "clients," which gives listeners even more space.

Summary of tips for "compare"

- One reason prospects may want to talk with you is to compare what you offer to what they currently have.

- Mention other people (e.g., clients, business owners, people about to retire) but do not add "like you." This helps reduce push-back by giving prospects space.

- Avoid wording that sounds like prospects *should* compare because that usually backfires. Instead, say they *may* want to compare.

- Remember to use "and" in place of "but."

- Remember to check in with the prospect using a direct question.

- Though I've provided examples of counters that give a reason to compare, using this approach can be too narrow. I suggest first trying the approach that doesn't mention a reason.

How to counter with "complement"

This time I'll begin with tips and important concepts about this approach for handling objections.

The central idea for this counter is your products or services would coexist with their current providers, not supplant them.

Do not use this counter if having two or more providers tends to create problems for the customer or your company.

The approach only works well when you genuinely embrace the idea of co-existence. If you try to use this as a foot in the door, things will likely fall apart once you get into the sales conversation.

Examples of using this counter are shown below. Notice they use the same best practices of mentioning others, as well as using the word "and."

Examples of using "complementary"

Prospect says, "My *assistant does that.*"

You counter with, "Many clients have us partner with their assistants because our services tend to mesh well at that level. Shall we see if this would be the case for you and your assistant, too?"

Prospect says, "Our HR department is doing an excellent job."

You reply, "We work very closely with those in HR and consider them important stakeholders. In fact, I often meet with management and HR at the same time to explore a potential fit. How does that sound to you?"

Prospect says, "We're happy with our bank."

You say, "We have a number of clients who work with a couple banks because the services fit well together. Shall we see if that might be the case for your company, too?"

Prospect says, "We handle that in-house."

You say, "Many clients have excellent in-house services and use us as-needed. For example, when their department is booked or they need extra resources. Can we see if this might be a good fit for you, too?"

Complement to earn the business?

I just cautioned against using this approach as a sneaky foot in the door because that tends to backfire. However, it can be effective if you remove the sneaky part.

Prospect says, "We've been with our accountants for ten years."

You counter with, "Many people I talk with have long-standing relationships. And decide to meet with me to see if my expertise complements existing services. *I see this as a way to demonstrate value and potentially earn the entire business.* Is this something you'd be open to exploring?"

More tips for "complement"

One reason prospects may want to talk with you is to see if your products/services work well with (complement) what they already have. There are many aspects of a complementary existence:

You may cover just some locations, you may have products or expertise the other guys do not (and vice versa), you may step up as-needed. Some companies limit contract amounts per provider, some want to hire locally in addition to national vendors. Some managers want to test new providers, some don't like the current vendor but don't want to make waves with a full change, some like to play vendors against each other...

Those are just a handful of reasons why a prospect may like a complementary approach. Alas, we can't make precise predictions so it's often best to use a general reference, as shown in the above examples.

That said, some callers find it's effective to reference specific ways products/services may complement. If you do this, use only things you genuinely support (do not try to guess what prospects will like).

As with the other approaches:

- Mention other people but do not add "like you." (i.e., say "business owners," not "business owners like you"). This helps reduce push-back by giving prospects space.

- Avoid wording that sounds like prospects *should* use complementary products or services. Instead, simply say they *may* find this works well.

- Remember to use "and" in place of "but."

- If you see this as a foot in the door, say that upfront.

- Remember to check in with the prospect using a direct question.

How to counter with "just in case"

Even though they're happy, there's a third reason prospects may want to talk with you: to have a known option in case things change.

Their wants and needs may change. Current providers and practices may no longer do a good job. Experts retire. Companies go out of business or are merged out of existence. Technology and tools change. New resources become available. Bosses and their preferences change...this list could go on.

Examples of using "just in case"

Prospect says, "We've got a broker."

You counter with this, *"That's true for most people I talk with. Many decide to sit down with me so they have an option in case things change. How does that sound to you?"*

Prospect says, "We've been working with the same printer for 15 years."

You reply, *"I just spoke with a fellow who has used the same shop for a long time, too. He decided to give me a chance to describe our services so he'd have an option. In case things change, his printer retires, and so on. How about talking on a just in case basis?"*

Prospect tells you, "We don't need a website beyond what we've got now. Besides, I like working on it."

You say, *"A lot of consultants say the same thing. Many decide to chat with me as a sort of safety net, in case things change and they want to delegate. Shall we talk on that basis?"*

More tips for "in case"

- We can't predict what kind of change may resonate with each prospect, so it's often best to leave things open. e.g., *"In case things change"* instead of "In case rates increase too much."

- That said, some callers include a type of change. As long as it makes sense to you—as opposed to trying to psych prospects out—this can work well, too.

- Be careful about your mindset. If you try to use this as a foot in the door, things will likely fall apart once you get into the sales conversation.

- Use the same best practices as for other approaches; such as mentioning others, and using "and" in place of "but."

TIP: Use a good story

One of the examples above includes *"I just spoke with a fellow who..."* The idea behind this kind of statement is to lay groundwork to offer a counter without putting the prospect on the spot. You may wonder if this method should only be used if you really did just speak with such a fellow.

Don't stretch the truth too far, but as Mark Twain said, don't let the facts get in the way of a good story. If you spoke with someone at some point, or your colleague did, or you read about it (including in this book), or you can imagine it happening—use it.

Two more objection situations

There are a couple more situations which involve objections stated in specific ways. I've shown these separately because handling them often requires a different approach.

"We're too small, not ready, etc."

In this type of objection, it almost seems like the prospect thinks we're too good for them, saying things like:

"We're too small for a retirement plan."

"I couldn't possibly afford..."

"Sounds great but I'm not ready for that kind of..."

When you hear objections like those, do not respond by assuring them they are not too small, can certainly afford it, are absolutely ready, and so on. As kindly as you may mean it, making those assurances is still arguing, which won't work well. In addition, the prospect may be right about being a poor fit and you don't want to waste their time (or your own).

When you hear objections like those, acknowledge the issue and see if the prospect wants to discuss things at a high level right now. For example:

Prospect says, "I'd love to do that but we can't afford it."

You reply, *"You might be surprised. Can we talk a bit now and see where things go from there?"*

Prospect says, "We're too small for a retirement plan."

You say, *"We work with a wide range of companies. A brief conversation would tell us if there may be value for yours. Shall we chat now and go from there?"*

The idea is to have a brief discussion to explore the possible fit at a high, general level. If things look good, explain what you see as possible value (very generally), and ask for a separate and full sales conversation.

To use this approach, you need to be ready for that high-level discussion. Prepare a handful of questions which can clarify the general issues; e.g., questions to clarify whether the company is or is not 'big enough' for a retirement plan. See the Qualifying section for tips on identifying the issues and creating questions.

You also need to be ready to position that possible fit without trying to close a deal (it's way too early for that), and ready to ask for a sales conversation. And you need to be ready to bow out gracefully if things do not look good.

In short: create scripts that cover all of the above and have them handy when you make calls.

NAP or just a bit cranky?

The second type of objection to cover is when prospects express strong negative opinions, such as:

"I don't buy the idea that..."

"That sounds like a waste of money."

You can choose to move on when you hear statements like that. You can also choose to see if they're open to discussing things. For example:

Prospect says, "All banks are alike."

You say, *"Unfortunately, I hear that a lot. We're proud of the way we help our clients. Of course, whether we'd provide better value to you depends on a number of things. You willing to talk things over and go from there?"*

By saying, *"I hear that a lot,"* you acknowledge what the prospect said without agreeing with it (and therefore compromising your true opinion).

As shown above, you also need to put reality on the table: the only way the prospect can find out if your bank is different is to fully explore the fit. Because of this reality—and because this time you do want to push a bit—it's best to use "you."

In this situation, you're asking for a separate sales conversation, so you don't need to have questions ready.

In this situation, you're also seeing if the prospect is open to discussing things or is NAP: Not a Prospect. Be ready to move forward with prospects who are open, and be ready to let go of prospects who are not.

More Tips for Handling Objections

LET'S WRAP THIS section with more tips to help you succeed in handling vague and specific objections.

Create a quick reference for all objections

The best way to prevent feeling thrown by objections is to prepare to handle them. Use the tips and examples from this section to create a reference that shows your prepared responses for common objections.

DO NOT include this reference in with other scripts. Create a completely separate reference for handling objections.

Keep your reference handy while you make calls so you can easily use it. I encourage you to use it on paper, not on screen, because even one click-through slows responses down and may make you sound a bit canned.

<u>One</u> try

Your quick reference will show several options for handling objections. Do not let this draw you into annoying the heck out of prospects by trying to handle objections three times.

Use just one option or counter per prospect, even if their objection changes or they bring up a whole new objection. Try once, and let go as needed.

How to let go for now

Imagine the prospect had a specific objection. You offered a counter but it was not accepted. Just because the prospect didn't open the door this time, that doesn't mean you're out of luck forever. How do you put luck on your side? You call again!

Use the same call-back strategy, e.g., "Well, thanks for chatting with me about that. I'd like to check in again at some point. Is that okay?"

Note: Use Step 2 of the call-back strategy, if you wish. However, do not use Step 3 even when the prospect gives you a specific-sounding timeframe. You already pushed them a bit by countering their objection, asking another nosy question is probably too much.

When there is no high-level fit

Imagine the prospect said something like this, "I don't think I'd qualify for private banking."

You countered by suggesting they may be surprised, and asked if they were willing to chat about it. The prospect agreed, shared information with you and it turns out there is <u>not</u> a high level fit.

Along with questions you'll ask to explore the fit at a high level, your quick reference should include at least one way to bow out gracefully.

What bowing-out sounds like varies quite a bit depending on the industry and target market. Here's a couple examples to help you get started on your own:

If the private banker determines the prospect does not qualify she says, *"Thanks for answering those questions. Sounds like the bells and whistles we offer wouldn't have value and could even add cost to your banking. But do you have any questions for me before we say so long?"*

If the shipping rep determines the prospect does not ship enough for a dedicated account manager and discounts, he says, *"I sure appreciate you taking time to talk with me. The shipping volume fits the retail options the best. They do a great job. Can I tell you where your nearest stores are?"*

Notice the callers thank prospects for their time and/or information—it's the polite thing to do.

Notice the callers are clear on the lack of a fit but word things differently. The first caller is honest about the probability private banking would actually cost more (and leaves out the fact they wouldn't qualify). The second caller is honest, too, but focuses on what does fit best, which happens to be elsewhere (their retail shops).

Notice both callers offer something in return. This is not only polite, it turns calls into networking. By offering and giving assistance, the callers make a good impression. The people they spoke with spread the word, and doors remain open.

Tips on following through

I covered a number of objection-counters that involve follow-through. Here are tips to help you succeed with those next steps.

Use follow *through*, not follow up

This tip is one of those subtle wording things that can make a big difference.

The phrase "follow up" implies the prospect asked you to do something. They did not ask you to do anything—they agreed to your request—and so the phrase will seem disingenuous.

Use following through instead, as in, "We spoke about five weeks ago and I sent you some links to videos about our program. *I'm following through.* Were you able to take a look?"

It's not about the item sent

Though the above example asks if the prospect had a chance to look at what was sent, be careful not to focus the call on the item. The objective is still to see if the prospect is open to exploring the business fit, so prepare scripts that segue from asking about the sent item to that.

Let's say the prospect told you they did indeed watch the videos. Your script might include something like, *"Tell me a bit about what jumped out at you."*

Do not try to script responses to prospects' answers to the above. There will be too much variety and trying to handle it all in print will clutter up your script.

Do script a segue from discussion to the point of your call, such as, *"I'd like the chance to explore a fit in greater depth. Can we set up a time to do that?"*

Of course, many prospects—maybe most of them—will not have read or seen what you sent. Your script should be ready for that, too. *"I know how it goes, I've got a stack of articles to read, myself. I'd like the chance to walk through our programs in terms of a possible fit for your group. Can we set up a time to do that?"*

In the next conversation, be true to the "just in case" agreement

Remember the three counters to specific objections are compare, complement, and just in case.

When prospects agree to compare, they have agreed to have a sales conversation.

When prospects accept the counter your products or services may complement and agree to discuss that, they have agreed to have a sales conversation.

When prospects expressed a strong negative opinion but agree to talk things over, they have agreed to have a sales conversation.

When prospects agree to talk "just in case," they <u>have not agreed</u> to have a sales conversation. In these situations, you both agreed to talk so they'd have another known option in case they want or need one. Prepare for the conversation on that basis.

It's also important to acknowledge this agreement as you start the next conversation, at the point I call "Set the Stage." Here's an example:

"Glad to have the chance to meet with you. When we spoke on the phone, you explained you're not in the market for a new broker, making this conversation informational. Is there anything in particular you want me to be sure to cover?"

Though some prospects will now indicate they are open to considering another broker (provider, CPA, supplier, etc.), do not depend on it. Instead—again, because it's important—be fully ready to proceed on an informational basis.

As the conversation proceeds: if the prospect indicates an interest in your products and services, check in to see if that's indeed the case. e.g., *"Sounds like the door is open for a competitive bid. Am I hearing that right?"*

If you're wrong, acknowledge with something like, *"Fair enough,"* and get back to your plan.

If you're right, switch gears to a full sales conversation (ask for more time or another meeting, if needed).

If your conversation has remained informational throughout: close the conversation by indicating your interest in having the chance to earn their business, and ask them for next steps. For example:

"Again, I'm glad to have the chance to talk. We'd love the opportunity to earn your business, as well. What would you like to do from here?"

Putting the ball in the prospect's court continues to demonstrate respect and qualifies them at the same time.

Key Points, and Next

It may be helpful to know vague objections are more common than specific objections. Be ready to use the call-back strategy quite a bit.

As for specific objections; it's important to counter without making assumptions or essentially telling the prospect they are paying too much, have the wrong thing, can do better, etc. When you put all of that aside, there are only three reasons why they may want to talk with you, anyway. Those reasons are:

- To compare

- To see if your products/services would complement

- To have an option in case things change

As you counter objections, acknowledge the issue because this actually defuses it. Use the word "and" to bridge between acknowledgment and the counter.

Give prospects space by talking about other people. e.g., "Business owners" or "homeowners," (not "homeowners like you." This helps prevent push-back.

Create a cheat sheet or quick reference for handling objections. Do not mush these into your other scripts.

When a prospect has an objection, try to counter it once; any more, and you're likely to annoy prospects and waste your own time.

Next up, what to do when you do not reach prospects or gatekeepers live on the phone. That's right—it's time to cover voicemail.

VOICEMAIL

Wading Through the Advice

Two Valid Schools of Thought

Why Voicemail is a Verbal Postcard

Effective Message Formats

Avoiding Common Errors

Leaving Messages That Get Returned

You gotta take a chance to have a chance.

(Advice from every coach in the entire history of sports)

Familiar (Bad) Advice

ASK FOR ADVICE about voicemail and you're likely to hear the same things we hear about cold calling in general.

Some say leaving messages is a waste of time. They may even tell you they tried it and "nobody" called them back. Their poor results are probably due to assumptive or rambling messages, and unrealistic expectations.

You may be told you need a compelling solution statement, or that a teaser is the way to go. The first is assumptive, the second is manipulative, both backfire.

You may hear the "six calls" myth yet again, as in you need to leave six messages before they call you back. That's as untrue for voicemail as it is for other calls.

You may also hear that when prospects call you back that means they are very interested. This is similar to the idea prospects who take your call are extra-hot prospects—and just as erroneous.

Some will assert the importance of always leaving messages, others will say never leave messages. Both of these opinions are actually correct!

Two schools of thought

There are two valid schools of thought for leaving voicemail messages:

- One approach is to skip leaving voicemails and keep calling until live humans answer.

- The other approach sees voicemail as a marketing opportunity—and so of course we should leave messages.

Each of these are valid, effective ways to go. I'll start with the do-not-leave-messages approach.

When skipping voicemail

With this approach, you just hang up when you get prospects' voicemail and dial the next call.

Skipping voicemail is a good option when you have thousands and thousands of prospects to call. With so many prospects, you can put luck on your side by making lots of calls to different prospects, potentially calling each prospect just once.

Skipping voicemail is also a good option when you have hundreds and hundreds of prospects to call—as long as you have tools to make re-calling them easy. With this size list, you'll need to call prospects more than once to put luck on your side.

Though you can just cycle through the list over and over, it's best to vary the day of the week and time you re-call prospects. There are many software tools to help you do this; however, you'll need one that truly makes it easy by requiring as few clicks as possible. (Hint: run screaming away from most CRM, shop for dialer programs instead.)

Does it make sense to automate?

There are two types of automation you may want to consider: predictive dialers, and dialers.

Predictive dialers dial automatically, "predict" a live human has answered the call, and connect you at that point. Most include features that let you prerecord a message that will be left on prospects' voicemail .

If you have several thousands to call, a predictive dialer may be just the ticket. However, these systems have their downside (including only *predicting* a live human is on the line). In general, you need lists with over 3,000 numbers, and two callers, for a predictive dialer to do its thing efficiently.

A plain "dialer" spares you from punching in the phone number. These, too, often include features for prerecording a voicemail message so you can leave it at the click of a mouse.

There is no minimum for using dialers, but make sure they include tickler features so you can vary the next day/time for calls.

Beware of frustration

Whether you use a system or not, if you start equating voicemail to "bad" calls, you'll get frustrated, which will pull down performance.

Pay attention to how you feel. If you start getting frustrated, apply the second school of thought and leave messages.

Voicemail messages equal marketing

The second school of thought for voicemail messages sees them as a terrific marketing opportunity. Here's why:

- Leaving messages is an excellent way to build name or brand awareness.

- Leaving messages helps support a relationship-based approach because your focus isn't on just those prospects who happen to pick up the phone.

- You can use that message space as if it's your own radio ad or mini-podcast—how cool is that!?

Another way to think of voicemail messages is as verbal postcards. This is an excellent analogy because the response rate for voicemail—3% or so—is roughly the same as for postcards.

Why "low" response has high value

You may look at that response rate and wonder if leaving voicemail messages is worth the effort because we can't be sure people will even listen to our messages.

On the one hand, that's precisely why some people do not leave messages at all.

On the other hand, would we not send emails or letters because we can't be sure prospects will read them? Would we pass on buying billboard space or radio ads because we can't be certain prospects will see or listen to them?

No, we'd go for it! We'd use those marketing tools as effectively as possible, including weighing factors like cost, effort, and response rates—the same applies to leaving messages.

In addition, voicemail messages tend to have greater impact than letters, email, radio and so on. One reason behind this greater impact is listeners know leaving them requires effort and are often favorably impressed. (This goes double, considering today's robo-messages.)

Another reason behind the increased impact is due to the personal touch—our voice and what we say. So let's turn to how we make that impact.

Voicemail Formats

THERE ARE TWO message formats. The unconventional format simply adds something at the end of the message.

<u>Standard Format</u>

Who you are

Phone number

Why you're calling

Call to action

Name and number

<u>Unconventional Format</u>

Who you are

Phone number

Why you're calling

Call to action

"in the meantime..."

Tip, ad, tidbit or quote

Voicemail and other scripts share many best practices already covered, so this time I'll walk through their elements and common errors at the same time.

It's the same Who You Are

Both message formats start with saying who you are. Apply the same guidelines as for other scripts; in fact, most callers find they can use the exact same wording.

Phone number

Next is your phone number. Sharing this upfront makes it easier for prospects to replay and get that information. (In contrast, prospects have to be highly motivated to replay and wait for the end of the message.)

TIP: Leave just one number, not your office phone and other office phone and assistant's phone, and mobile number...

It's the same Why You're Calling

After stating the phone number, say why you're calling. This is where a lot of voicemails fail, for the same reasons contact/prospect calls backfire. To avoid errors, follow the same guidelines for consultative calls. In fact, Why You're Calling may come from other scripts with minimal or no adjustment.

TIP: It's absolutely okay to use the same exact wording you'd use when talking with live humans (few prospects, if any, will notice).

Avoiding errors with the Call to Action

After saying why you're calling, it's time to make a "call to action." There are a number of errors people often make with this—and one simple solution—so I'll go over the errors first.

Error number one is skipping a Call to Action entirely. People who make this error often believe interested prospects will jump into action on their own. There is some truth to this, and we see it when prospects return our call because they just happened to be looking at that time. Alas, this is needle-in-haystack rare.

The vast majority of prospects who hear our message have low to middling interest for a variety of reasons, but are still open to talking with us. However, without a Call to Action, these prospects won't be paying enough attention to be inspired to call us back (I'll explain why in a bit).

Error number two is using the word "if." For example, "If you're interested, please call me back." We tend to say things like that in an effort to be polite. However, including "if you're interested" and similar statements often result in zero return calls.

Error number three is including "at your convenience." This, too, is usually an attempt to be respectful. This, too, usually reduces return calls to zero.

There's a much better way to be polite and still generate return calls. Before I share that with you, I want to cover a couple techniques that simply backfire: teasers and implied threats.

A teaser is something like this, "Did you know you can save up to 36% on your energy bill? Call me back to find out how!" Many prospects find this approach insulting.

An implied threat sounds like, "I'm calling from your bank. Please call me about your accounts." Implied threats do actually generate return calls, but as soon as prospects realize it was a ploy, efficacy and the caller's credibility take a nose-dive.

Why some respectful calls to action don't work

Let's go back to those polite calls to action and why they don't help generate return calls.

We and our prospects live and work in a world full of noise and distraction. On our end of the line, we're pretty focused on making calls.

On our prospects' end of the line, they're dealing with noise and distraction by paying less attention to some stuff, including voicemail messages. They tend to pay less attention to messages from strangers. They also pay less attention to compound statements, such as "Call me if you're interested" and statements that include "at your convenience."

That's why polite calls to action don't work well. To give ourselves the best chance of return calls, we need to stand out among the distraction.

The most effective call to action

We don't want to use disingenuous teasers or implied threats. To stand out in a good way, voicemail messages need something clean and simple.

Here is the most effective Call to Action—the words that generate actual return calls: *"Please give me a call."* That's all there is to it!

Here are more versions:

"Please call me at 510 555 1234."

"Please call me, Shawn Greene, at 510 555 1234."

Now let's go back to the voicemail formats.

Closing the message: Standard format

In review, the whole format is:

- Who you are
- Phone number
- Why you're calling
- Call to action
- Name and number

In the standard voicemail format, you close the message by repeating your name and phone number. This spares prospects from having to hit 'replay' at all.

TIP: You gave one phone number at the beginning of the message. Feel free to give a different number at the end. However, say just one number each time.

Closing the message: Unconventional format

Both voicemail formats are the same up to the point of saying a Call to Action. With the unconventional voicemail format, you segue from the Call to Action into <u>one</u> of the following:

- A tip
- A quote
- Tidbit or trivia
- An ad

The idea is to use the end of the message-space more creatively. Many who use this format report they get a greater number of return calls. Using this format also prevents boredom for the caller because the messages are more interesting to work with.

Concerns about being unconventional

I have to acknowledge lots of workshop and webinar participants express initial concerns about using this format.

Some worry adding a bit of trivia will seem unprofessional. Some think it's going to be too hard to come up with a tip, much less one the compliance department will approve. The idea of using an ad worries some callers—won't that seem pushy? Others worry using a quote even from someone as serious as Abraham Lincoln may seem unserious.

Many of your peers—from the most junior rep to senior account executives—find the format works quite well. If you were in training with me, I'd encourage you to play with this option in class and then decide. I still advise you to try it before deciding, even though you'll do that with real messages.

Now let's take a look at each less-conventional option.

Using a Tip

The best kind of tip is one that shows off your (or your company's) expertise. The second best is a tip related to your business or industry. The third most effective tip is one that is topical or timely. Any of those help your message stand out in good ways, and even help build relationships because you're sharing something of value.

It's important to use tips people can apply on their own. If they have to talk to you to get the full story, it's not a tip, it's a teaser.

The bad news is that it can indeed be tough to come up with tips that fit in a voicemail message (compliance may slow things down, too). However, the effort can be doubly valuable because you can also use these tips in place of boring elevator speeches.

Using a Quote

Using quotes is definitely the most popular choice of all the options. Quotes can be inspirational, funny, famous, unusual, motivational—there's a huge range and that makes them ideal for almost everyone's voicemail messages.

Quotes with some sort of connection to your work can be particularly effective. However, using one just because you like it has also proven to be effective, probably because it conveys something about your personality.

In general, stay away from political or religious quotes. The exception is when you are working in politics or religion.

Using Tidbits or Trivia

Technically, a "tidbit" is a tiny morsel of information. Its root means a delicious piece of information, which may be where we got the expression "juicy gossip."

See that? That's a tidbit! Trivia is very similar but often focuses on facts some may find inconsequential (trivial). These are sometimes called "factoids," by the way.

It's not important to know which is which and both are easy to find, making them ideal for including in messages. You may want to use tidbits related to your industry, or area, or something topical; however, this is not vital for messages to be effective.

Historical trivia is particularly easy to find and use. Just search "today in history" and you'll find a bunch.

Stay away from tidbits like "40% of business owners are under-insured." These come across as lecturing and self-centered. Be careful about using statistics, too, because 53% of prospects will think you invented them. (By the way, I invented both of those statistics.)

As with quotes; be careful with political or religious trivia that has too strong a connection to current events. However, events from long ago are usually safe if you don't add too much opinion to them.

For example: "Joan of Arc was made a saint this month, 489 years after being burned at the stake" is okay.

"At the age of just 19, Joan of Arc was brutally murdered by money-grubbing, power-mad church leaders" is not okay.

Using an Ad

An ad is a shameless plug for your expertise, company, upcoming seminar, products, and so on. Part of what makes using ads acceptable and effective is telling listeners what it is upfront. For example, *"...here's an ad for our upcoming seminar."*

Speaking of something that tells listeners what comes next...

From the Call to Action to Ad, Tidbit, Tip or Quote

Because I just covered something out of order, here's the unconventional format again:

- Who you are

- Phone number

- Why you're calling

- Call to action

- "in the meantime..."

- Tip, tidbit, trivia, quote, ad

In the unconventional format, you state a Call to Action and then add a tip, tidbit, quote, or ad. To avoid sounding awkward you need a segue—a statement that bridges from Call to the next part.

That segue often starts with, *"In the meantime,"* which is why that phrase is shown in the format. I'll show you several examples in a bit; first, I need to address the optional repeat of name and phone number.

No name and number again?

Many people are accustomed to saying their name and phone number at the end of a voicemail message. Most get how saying the number earlier works well, but the idea of *only* saying it at the beginning can seem strange.

You really, truly only need to say your name and number at the beginning and that's why they're not shown at the end of the unconventional format. However, repeating those at the end won't hurt.

Analyze the Other Guys' Messages

LOOKING AT OTHER callers' voicemail messages is a great way to see what to avoid—and what to do instead—so it's time again to analyze the other guys. We'll start with our private banker's message.

A private banker's original (ineffective) voicemail

This is Rochelle from the downtown office of Excalibur Bank Wealth Management. We provide outstanding service to all our clients.

I'd like to talk with you about your banking and investment needs.

If you're interested in joining our exclusive wealth management group, please call me back.

Again, this is Rochelle. Wealth Management. 510 555 1234. Our website is www.ExcaliburWealth.com.

"Outstanding" service?

Actually, before I cover that phrase let's start with how Rochelle says who she is:

She needs a pause (a comma) before she says where she works. The sentence is also on the long side because it uses a high number of syllables. It's long for me, that is, try it aloud to see if you can say it all in one easy breath.

After saying who she is, Rochelle mentions providing "outstanding service." She's using that as a value proposition, but since clients expect excellent service as a given, mentioning it will sound odd.

I also want you to know you do not need any sort of value proposition for these messages to generate return calls. In fact, if you want to highlight value, use the unconventional format.

Just wants to chat?

Rochelle says she wants to talk about needs. But her prospects know she doesn't only want to chat and the unstated agenda will undermine results.

The "if" also jumps ahead

Rochelle uses "if" in her call to action, which weakens its effect quite a bit. By referring to "joining," she also jumps ahead into selling—an assumption most prospects will reject.

Be careful with words like "exclusive"

Rochelle describes the private banking group as "exclusive." This is accurate, but the word will appeal only to some and turn others off.

If Rochelle specifically wants prospects who like the idea, using "exclusive" will be effective. If she's trying to have broader appeal she should not use benefit-type words, especially that one.

What's with the website?

At the end of the message, Rochelle mentions their website. She needs to add a reason to look at it, otherwise, there's no context.

Rochelle may also be able to subtract the triple-w. The shorter the message, the better, and many prospects will understand a URL without it.

Standard format for Rochelle's message

Let's fix Rochelle's message so she gets return calls.

WHO: This is Rochelle. I'm part of the wealth management team for Excalibur Bank.

PHONE: 510 555 1234.

WHY CALLING: I'd like to see if our services are a good fit for you.

CALL TO ACTION: Please call me back.

NAME AND PHONE NUMBER: Again, this is Rochelle. 510 555 1234. For general information about our services, see ExcaliburWealth.com.

Tips about stating location

The revised message does not mention being in the downtown office. Here are tips to help decide whether you want to mention location or not:

- If there are so many locations that prospects may easily confuse one with another, mentioning location can be helpful.

- It's also helpful to mention location if you are local and compete with non-local companies.

- If you have an accent often associated with off-shore call centers—but you are local—be sure to mention your location.

Tips about a website at the end

The revised message adds a reason to look at the website, *"For general information about our services."* There's no triple-w because most of Rochelle's prospects don't need to hear that part. (I should also note the voicemail format does not include mentioning a website. The primary reason is because having a website is no longer remarkable—*not* having one is.)

Unconventional format for Rochelle's message

This format comes with several options. Rochelle uses a tip.

WHO YOU ARE: This is Rochelle. I'm part of the wealth management team for Excalibur Bank.

PHONE NUMBER: 510 555 1234.

WHY YOU'RE CALLING: I'd like to see if our services are a good fit for you.

CALL TO ACTION: Please call me back.

TIP: In the meantime, here's a banking services tip. Do you have photo negatives you haven't had a chance to scan? Store them securely in your safe deposit box.

By the way, our clients have their safe deposit box fees waived. That's just one benefit. I'll be happy to go over the rest.

Notice what's the same

The message is the same from Who, to the Call to Action. What makes it unconventional is what comes next—a tip, in this case.

Tips about using Tips

Remember to bridge from the Call to Action with something like, *"In the meantime..."* (That phrase tends to fit with most tips, quotes, etc.)

Rochelle's tip is about banking services in general, giving it broad appeal and applicability. This is an excellent approach when calling a broad range of prospects.

Remember compound sentences don't come through very well. This is why the message is not, "If you have photo negatives you haven't had a chance to scan, store them in your safe deposit box." (That's an awfully long sentence, anyway.)

Want to avoid using a compound sentence? Make the first part into a question, as shown in this paragraph and the above example script.

Making the link obvious

Rochelle closes her message by mentioning a specific benefit. She goes on to say there are more benefits (of course) and she'll be happy to go over them.

That kind of link is ideal but not always possible. Work on tips you can link directly to your services, but don't worry if you can't come up with one—using tips still works very well.

What's not in the message

Rochelle does not say her name and phone number at the end of the message because it's not needed. You may want to complete a brief exercise to see what that's like on both ends of the phone line:

- Call your own number and leave Rochelle's message using the example as shown above. As you leave the message, you may feel something is missing. Ignore it—that's just a feeling of doing something differently.

- Listen to the message next. Does it sound strange without her name and number at the end? What happens if you hit replay to get that info?

There's no right or wrong here. If you really think name and number should be repeated, here's what it looks like, *"...I'll be happy to go over the rest. Rochelle. 510 555 1234."*

That's it—just name and number. Any more and you run the risk of a message that's too long and sounds a bit rambling.

A printing rep's original (ineffective) message

Our next example to analyze comes from a fellow who sells printing and related services.

"Hello. My name is Justin Timberlake and I work for an AMAZING printing company called Print World Inc. As a Member of our Chamber of Commerce, you are entitled to a FREE, no obligation review of your collaterals, annual reports, and so on.

We can use this review to see how our services will help you. So call me back right away while this offer is available.

I am Justin Timberlake. My numbers are 510 555 1234 and 925 555 4567. Have a great day!"

Pros and cons of a famous name

"Justin Timberlake" is currently a well-known name with positive connotation (mostly).

On the upside for our caller, using his full famous name may prompt stronger attention. On the downside, prospects may pay less attention to what comes next as they wonder if they heard the name right.

Those pros and cons are equal, so Justin should apply his own preference for using his full name or just his first. The exception to this guideline: if the famous name acquires a negative connotation, drop the last name.

Perky superlatives and CAPS

Justin's original message is pretty darn perky. That's a good fit for his personality, so he should stick with it. However, those all-caps should go, for the same reasons they're not used in other scripts.

Free no obligation assumption

Justin's message centers on a review of the prospect's marketing and other printed stuff. He says it's free, which may or may not be worth stating.

If that kind of thing is normally free, highlighting "free" can sound unprofessional or disingenuous.

If that kind of thing is not usually free (or if it varies a lot) then saying it's free is a good idea.

Justin goes on to say the review has no obligation. Since most prospects expect there's no obligation, the statement tends to sound unprofessional or even sneaky. This problem is compounded by Justin assumptively saying the print company "will" help the prospect.

Faux limitation

There's no real time limit for this nifty review and most prospects know that. Most prospects also know the review is free for anyone, not just Chamber members. This stretching of the truth can undermine results.

Two numbers in the wrong place

Justin closes his message by sharing two phone numbers. It almost works because he says, "My numberS are..."

However, few (or zero) prospects will bother to note both numbers. Besides, won't Justin respond to a call on either number? Of course he will, and that's why one phone number is plenty.

Standard format for Justin's message

WHO YOU ARE: My name is Justin Timberlake and I work for an amazing printing company called Print World.

PHONE NUMBER: 510 555 1234

WHY YOU'RE CALLING: We'd like to see if our print shop could help your company succeed and shine.

CALL TO ACTION: Please give me a call.

NAME AND NUMBER: I'm Justin Timberlake, though not the famous one. My mobile is 925 555 4567. Have a great day!

What's the same, what's different

Justin really believes the company is amazing and he's an upbeat guy. Keeping those elements in the message helps draw the right prospects to him, and can help keep his energy high (though he may not need help). The all-caps are gone. So is the "Inc," because the company name is far more important than its business entity.

TIP: Why you don't have to say "LLC," etc.

Certain business entities carry rules about including acronyms with the company name. For example, if a company is formed as a LLC, we're supposed to show that on written materials and websites. The same is true when the business is incorporated.

However, there's leeway to those rules. For example, Amazon's name is technically "Amazon.com, Inc." but we don't see that front and center on its website.

What's more, the rules do not apply to spoken words—in your voicemail messages—so feel free to leave the entity acronym out.

Back to notes: Let your personality shine through

Have I mentioned how upbeat Justin is? His ebullient nature comes through in Why he's calling and makes it work; otherwise, it would sound fake.

Justin also leverages his name by explaining he's not the famous fellow. Again, this works because it suits his personality and natural way of talking, but may not work for other callers.

Pros and cons of using two numbers

Sharp-eyed readers may notice Justin's message has one phone number at the beginning and a different number at the end.

The downside is some prospects will hear two different numbers, spend a nanosecond wondering which one to use—then choose not to call either of them.

On the other hand, some callers feel using two numbers gives them double the chance of a return call. If you want to test this for yourself, I suggest using a mobile number for the second one and identifying it as such (as shown in the example).

If you'd like a crystal clear recommendation: use one phone number.

Unconventional format on next page...

Unconventional format for Justin's message

Justin has collected a ton of tidbits about printing, paper, and other things related to his business. He uses just one tidbit per message, like this one:

WHO YOU ARE: My name is Justin Timberlake and I work for an amazing printing company called Print World.

PHONE NUMBER: 510 555 1234

WHY YOU'RE CALLING: We'd like to see if our print shop could help your company succeed.

CALL TO ACTION: Please give me a call.

TIDBIT: In the meantime, here's a note from my printing nerd files. A serif font is one that has little lines at the bottom and sometimes the top of vertical marks. These were created hundreds of years ago by monks who wanted to avoid drawing raggedy looking letters. We don't like raggedy looking print, either, and make sure our clients' materials shine.

Notes about this example voicemail

Most of the first half of the message is the same as the standard version but there's one difference. In this version Justin says, *"help your company succeed"* but leaves out *"and shine."* This frees him to use "shine" at the end of the message.

Keep that example in mind as you create your own messages. We often come up with a phrase we like, then get stuck on how to avoid repeating it in the same message. See if you can use just part of the phrase, or find alternate words in your favorite thesaurus.

Justin's message does not repeat his name and number at the end. To help you evaluate this approach, I'm not going to show an example that adds it.

More notes & tips for using trivia and tidbits

When we use trivia and tidbits, our first instinct may be to say, "Did you know?" (e.g., "Did you know monks invented serif fonts?") Including a rhetorical question often makes the message longer, so try to avoid them.

Justin doesn't call his tidbit a "tidbit" or "factoid," he calls it a note from his printing nerd files. This, too, lets his personality come through—which is a good thing. You should feel free to call these what you wish, too.

Justin also ties the tidbit to the business, which helps the business context stand out.

The last tip has to do with projecting the image we wish to convey. Let's imagine our Justin Timberlake is more serious-minded. Some wordsmithing will make the same tidbit work for him, especially if he leaves his famous last name out of the message:

My name is Justin and I work for a printing company called Print World. 510 555 1234. We'd like to see if our services would provide value to your company. Please give me a call.

In the meantime, here's a bit of printing history. A serif font is one that has little lines at the bottom and sometimes the top of vertical marks. These were created hundreds of years ago by monks who wanted crisp, clean, elegant lettering.

We apply the same careful attention to our clients' printed materials.

A consultant's original (bad) voicemail message

Next is Richard Sanderburg, a marketing consultant. Like many service-providers, he occasionally holds seminars to demonstrate his expertise and build his network. Here's his original message:

"This is Richard Sanderburg ABC Marketing Services. We're holding a seminar on using social media and SEO myths on Thursday, April 18th, in the Westville Community Center auditorium.

You are cordially invited to attend and bring a guest to this valuable, informative and interactive program.

If you would like to reserve your seats, contact my assistant, Lulu Dietz, at 707 555 1234. That's Lulu Dietz, D I E T Z."

Who should make the calls?

I'll start with the close of Richard's message. The main contact is someone other than the person leaving the message. This adds a layer which will require effort to decipher—not a ton of effort, but enough to turn many prospects off. Richard should ask prospects to call him, or Lulu should make the calls.

More critique, from the top

Richard made his company name part of his last name. He needs a comma—a pause—between the two.

Concisely describing the seminar is great, but it sounds like it is about using SEO myths and I bet that's not what he means. There's also too much packed into that single sentence, making it too much to absorb, and too long to say in one breath. He needs to break that information into smaller sentences.

The cordial invitation to prospects and a guest is nice. However, describing the seminar as "valuable, informative and interactive" may backfire because attendees want to be the judge of that.

The call to action includes "if," which undermines the efficacy of the whole message.

I've already pointed out Richard should have people call him (or Lulu should call). I also want to point out there's no need for prospects to know how Lulu's last name is spelled.

About spelling a name

Brenden with two e's, Gerald with a g, Jon without an h, Jakob with a k...these are examples of names their owners often have to spell. However, spelling a name for prospects only makes sense if that helps prospects *hear* it.

Let's use a fellow named Jean (with French pronunciation) for example. If he's calling Canadians or people in most of Louisiana, his name will be relatively common and he probably does not need to spell it.

If he's calling areas in which that name is unfamiliar, spelling can help: *"Please call me back. 925 555 6789. My name is Jean. That's J. E. A. N. and rhymes with yawn."*

Also remember: it's not important prospects hear your name correctly—just close enough. If Jean's prospects ask for "Ron," Jean will know who they mean.

About spelling names for email reply

Sometimes callers want to include their email so prospects can respond that way, and sometimes that requires prospects to spell correctly.

On the one hand, this is a good reason for us to spell-out our email. On the other hand, there are 837 ways for that to go wrong; including annoying prospects, and misspelled emails that never get to us.

Do not expect that prospects will spell correctly. Use a phone number.

About spelling websites

Let's say Richard ended his voicemail with, "To reserve your seats, go to www.ABCmrktgserv.com and see the seminars tab." Good luck with prospects getting that one, right?

Here's the good news: search engines often show us URLs we're trying to type.

Here's the bad news: the correct website may not show up, and few prospects will work hard to find it.

The above paints yet another reason to use a phone number. However; if you really, really need to spell something, do it slowly and keep your expectations low.

Standard format for Lulu's message

Richard wants his assistant to handle seminar registration, so the examples are for her.

WHO YOU ARE: My name is Lulu and I'm with ABC Marketing Services.

PHONE NUMBER: 510 555 1234.

WHY YOU'RE CALLING: We're holding a seminar on using social media to boost business. I'd like to tell you more about the seminar and see if you'd like to attend.

CALL TO ACTION: Please give me a call.

NAME AND NUMBER: Again, my name is Lulu. 510 555 1234.

What's not in the message

Lulu's message doesn't mention SEO myths. Leaving that out makes room to add a mini benefit statement about using social media ("to boost business").

Richard's original voicemail went on to state a lot more information; including when the seminar would be held, where, people can bring a guest, the food that will be served (kidding on that last bit, but now I'm hungry). All of that makes the message too long and is not the point of the call, so it's gone, too.

Actually: There are two points to the call

One point of the call is to see if prospects want to attend the seminar. Most prospects won't agree without first hearing more about the seminar, so the other point is to ask for the opportunity to provide this information. Why You're Calling covers both of those points, just like it does in scripts for talking with live prospects.

A tip for unusual names

Lulu closes her message by saying, *"Again, my name is..."* Using "again" helps her remember to slow down before she says her unusual name, which also helps people hear it.

Unconventional format for Lulu's message

One of the options for this format is to have an ad at the end. Ads are perfect for sharing a lot of information, such as seminar information, so that's what Lulu uses.

Because the message itself will provide information, Why she's calling is slightly different from the standard format message above. Keep your eyes open for that difference.

WHO YOU ARE: "My name is Lulu and I'm with ABC Marketing Services.

PHONE: 510 555 1234

WHY YOU'RE CALLING: We're holding a seminar on using social media to boost business. We'd like to see if you'd like to attend.

CALL TO ACTION: Please give me a call.

AD: In the meantime, here's a bit about the seminar. Social media can be an excellent and inexpensive way to boost awareness of your business. Promote specials. And connect with customers. Our lead consultant, Richard Sanderburg, will share easy tips for using social media. He'll also cover how to avoid falling for expensive SEO myths.

The seminar will be on April 18th in the Westville Community Center auditorium. We'll start at 4 PM. Refreshments will be served. We'd love to have you and a guest attend.

Notes and tips about that message

Why You're Calling in this message barely says anything about the seminar itself. That's okay, because a half-second later prospects hear they can get more information if they listen to the rest of the message.

You may have noticed that's a longish message. Because it's long, Lulu says the most important stuff early in the ad and states the boring details (when, where, etc.) at the end.

We tend to do that the other way around when drafting messages about events: we start with details like when, how much, where to park, and so on. This kind of information is truly the boring details and should go last—flip your draft around, if needed.

Lulu closes the ad by saying, *"We'd love to have you and a guest attend."* That's a great way to close this particular message but for those of you who really, really want to repeat name and phone number, it looks like this: *"We'd love to have you and a guest attend. Give me a call to reserve your spots. Again, this is Lulu. 510 555 1234."*

The insurance broker's standard voicemail

I won't rip anything up this time. Let's focus on what works well, beginning with the standard format.

WHO YOU ARE: My name is Mary Hotsenpiller. I'm an expert in commercial insurance.

PHONE: 510 555 1234

WHY YOU'RE CALLING: I'd like to see if my expertise, and our special programs, would provide value to your company.

CALL TO ACTION: Please call me.

NAME AND NUMBER: 510 555 2345. If I'm not in, my assistant will be happy to take your message.

About that message

Mary chooses to include her last name in her messages. She likes the name and it's important to her. As long as she enunciates, this will work well.

The same applies to you, too. How you feel about using your last name is more important than whether your last name is hard for listeners to 'get' or not. (Because leveraging your personality is most effective.)

Mary adds a comment about her assistant at the end of the message. She does this because her firm has actual human assistants for their brokers. This seems to throw prospects off and they sometimes don't leave messages. The closing comment helps prevent this.

The insurance broker's unconventional format messages

Mary describes herself as conservative, and is certain using the unconventional format is not her style—nor her prospects' style.

Mary is just like many professionals who train with me. And, just like her peers, it takes her a while to warm up to the idea of leaving a less conventional message. What perks her willingness to try the format are the inspirational quotes she's got right on her office wall. (True story.)

WHO YOU ARE: My name is Mary Hotsenpiller. I'm an expert in commercial insurance.

PHONE: 510 555 1234

WHY YOU'RE CALLING: I'd like to see if my expertise, and our special programs, would provide value to your company.

CALL TO ACTION: Please give me a call.

QUOTE: In the meantime, I leave you with a quote from the father of fire insurance. Benjamin Franklin. "The constitution only gives people the right to pursue happiness. You have to catch it yourself."

Once she practiced, Mary decided she liked the format. Here's another:

WHO YOU ARE: My name is Mary Hotsenpiller. I'm an expert in commercial insurance.

PHONE: 510 555 1234

WHY YOU'RE CALLING: I'd like to see if my expertise, and our special programs, would provide value to your company.

CALL TO ACTION: Please give me a call.

QUOTE: In the meantime, here's one of my favorite quotes from Malcolm Forbes. 'Too many people overvalue what they are not and undervalue what they are.' I hope to have opportunity to discuss how we may help protect what you value. If I'm not in, my assistant will be happy to take your message.

Notes and tips for leaving quotes

Use quotes you like, not quotes you think prospects will like.

If you can, mention who said it. If using proverbs or sayings, mention that. e.g. *"In the meantime, I leave you with a Roman proverb. If there is no wind, row."*

Be careful with religious or political quotes.

When you can connect the quote to your business, do that. For example, there are a ton of quotes from Ben Franklin, who really did invent fire insurance. That connection makes his quotes perfect for insurance brokers, fire extinguisher and sprinkler systems salespeople, and lightening rod salespeople (do those still exist?).

However, it's okay if you cannot connect the quote to your business. Here's an example from Mary:

WHO YOU ARE: my name is Mary Hotsenpiller. I'm an expert in commercial insurance.

PHONE: 510 555 1234

WHY YOU'RE CALLING: I'd like to see if my expertise would provide value to your company.

CALL TO ACTION: Please give me a call.

QUOTE: In the meantime, here's one of my favorite quotes from Abraham Lincoln. "We can complain because rose bushes have thorns. Or rejoice because thorn bushes have roses."

There's no loop-back to her business at the end: she simply holds a beat and then hangs up.

Apply script-writing mode even to quotes, including using short sentences. For example, the above quote from Lincoln actually uses a comma instead of a period.

There's no need to punctuate your script with quotation marks. I only used them to clarify what's script and what's the quote.

About calling yourself...

Many people test their voicemail messages by calling their own number. When you listen to yourself, try not to be too critical. The way we hear ourselves is not how others hear us. In addition, because there is no live human on the other end, our messages tend to sound a little canned. That's okay! Listen for:

- Messages that fit in the space (not so long the end may be cut off).

- Clear speaking: slow down if needed. Shorten the message to help you do that, if needed.

Use your own voicemail, too

Now that you've read about alternatives for leaving messages, I invite you to consider using your outgoing message more effectively, too.

If you're on vacation or away for some other reason, tell us upfront. If there's someone else we can call, tell us that, too. However, we really don't need to hear you're away from your desk or helping others. We get that. Please do not say you'll return our call at "my earliest convenience"—we get that, too, but it sounds conceited.

Other than that, keep the main part short and have some fun with the rest! Include a tip, tidbit, quote, or ad for the latest and greatest.

Tips for your own outgoing message

See if your system lets callers skip the extra (e.g., by pressing pound or hashtag). If so, be sure to let callers know how to skip the extra before you get into it.

If your system does not allow callers to skip to where they can leave a message, do not add something at the end (makes the outgoing message too long).

Example

You've reached the office of Savage and Greene. This is Shawn speaking. I look forward to talking with you. This week's phone trivia follows. You can skip it by pressing pound.

The first telephone systems did not make a ringing sound for the caller. Phone companies soon realized many callers hung up because they thought the phone wasn't working.

A ring on the caller's end was added but it's not the same ring heard on the other end. That's why sometimes the other person picks up before we hear a ring.

Important: Choose one approach to voicemail

There are two valid approaches to voicemail messages. When your situation is such that either approach could fit, choose one or the other. Do not leave messages one day, skip leaving messages the next, leave messages for some prospects, skip it for others, etc.

Choosing one approach gives you the best opportunity to master that approach. Callers who use both—often based on mood—do not get very good results.

If you're not sure which you'll prefer

Run a test to see which approach works best for you:

- Test the approach in which you do not leave messages first. Use the approach for at least a couple months. (Unless you start feeling frustrated, in which case you should change to leaving messages.)

- Next, switch to leaving messages and use that approach for the same time period.

- Now compare your energy level throughout both periods, as well as number of calls made and percentage of contact with live prospects.

  If the contact rate is on the low end (25% or less), I recommend leaving messages so you get that marketing bump.

Summary, and Next

You're bound to encounter lots of voicemail (maybe even a few message machines). There are two valid approaches to handling messages.

One approach is to skip leaving messages: just keep calling until you reach a live human. This works well when you have several thousand on your list. It also works well if you have many hundreds on your list and the technology to make it easy to call again at another day and time.

The exception to the above is your own level of frustration. If you start to see getting prospects' voicemail as "bad" calls, use the other approach.

The other approach is to use voicemail as marketing opportunities. There are two voicemail formats in this case.

The standard format is as short as possible. Key elements are: An effective Why You're Calling (which may be exactly the same as in your other scripts) and a clear Call to Action.

The other format adds something at the end to make the message less conventional. This may be a quote, something resembling an ad, a bit of trivia or a tidbit, or a tip. Many people report a higher response rate with this format (over 5%, compared to the norm of 3%ish).

If you need to test which approach works best; start by skipping messages for a time, then leave messages for an equal period of time. Evaluate based on how you feel, number of calls, and contact rates.

Whichever approach to voicemail you use, you'll need to decide how many times to attempt to reach prospects. If you leave messages, you'll need to decide how many. Time to learn about this and other calling strategies.

STRATEGY

When To Call

How Often To Call

How Many Attempts

How Many Voicemails

What To Do When You Move On

If you don't know where you are going
you'll end up someplace else.

(Yogi Berra)

The Beauty of a System

OVERTHINKING MAKES TELEMARKETING much harder than it has to be. Sure, we should think about how we sound, which words to use, and even whether to use "Catherine" or "Cathy." However, continually and deeply pondering these things won't help (except as a nifty procrastination device).

The same is true for when to call, how often, and so on. Making these decisions prospect-by-prospect and call-by-call undermines success by adding effort and setting inappropriate expectations. Here's how:

When cold calling, we do not yet have enough information about prospects to make a sound judgement on the business fit or their value to us. But when we call certain prospects more often (or leave them more voicemails) that sends our brain the message these prospects are more important. This contradicts reality and reinforces inappropriate expectations, which leads to frustration.

When we think about calling some prospects more often and/or leaving more messages, we're also adding a bunch of small decisions onto the task of calling. As these little decisions pile up, our brain has less energy to handle the rest of what's involved—like talking with prospects.

In addition, as our thinking becomes fatigued, our emotions can grow out of proportion. A slight feeling of discouragement can snowball and overwhelm what's actually working well.

All of the above pull performance downward. What's more, the poor habits can become ingrained, making it harder to turn things around.

How a system prevents those problems

Using a system simply means thinking ahead to create your own guidelines, and then applying those guidelines. This prevents overthinking the little things, and supports success with less effort.

A system also helps you build positive, productive habits. Building these habits is the last piece of the puzzle—it's how cold calling goes from root-canal-ish to an effective marketing tool you can use whenever you want.

A system does not require strict adherence

Though creating and using a system is key to success, that doesn't mean the system should be rigid. The first system you define is not likely to be the last. As you make calls, gather data and analyze it, you'll probably adjust and refine your system. You'll need to do the same when market conditions or objectives change.

It's also important to know using a system does not mean sticking with it for every single situation no matter what. Using a system means you have more brain-space and energy to deal with what comes up—no matter what.

Some calls do not need a system

Before I cover the system, I want to clarify that it won't be used for all calls. The system described below applies to prospects you <u>have not</u> reached.

For prospects you have reached, define next steps based on their suggestion or preference or agreement.

The exception to the above is when you lose contact with prospects. For example: they suggested you call again in a few months, you do that, do not reach them, you try again, do not reach them...

You may want to manage next steps for those prospects on a case-by-case basis. However, many people find it's best to pop them back into the top of the funnel and apply the same system as for prospects who have not been reached.

The other type of call that doesn't need the system is related to list size. If you have many thousands of prospects to call; you don't need a system, you need to make a choice about voicemail messages:

Choose to leave voicemail messages or choose not to leave messages. Do one or the other for all prospects—do not pick and choose as you call.

System overview

The system is simple:

- Frequency (How often you will call prospects)
- Attempts (How many times you will try to reach prospects)
- Next (What happens next?)

The system also covers things like time of day, and days of the week. Including these elements is just as important for success but the particulars tend to be more variable.

TIP: Read first, define your system second

The chapters that follow cover each element, related tips, and best practices. You'll take it from there to set your own specifics, however, it may help to read and then circle back to define your system. To make that easy, I'll repeat the system elements near the end of this section.

How Often and How Many

THE KEY FACTORS in your strategy are how often you'll call prospects, and how many times you'll try to reach them.

Note: these and other factors in your system apply whether you're leaving voicemail messages or not.

Frequency (how often)

How often will you try to reach prospects? Weekly? Daily? Every nine days? Let's look at what may be too often, and what may not be often enough.

Calling too often

If you call too often you may seem over-eager or even desperate. Calling more than twice a week can put you in this category, calling daily probably will, too.

The above may not apply if you're using a predictive dialer (which only connect you to live answers) but not leaving messages. However, some prospects may be choosing not to answer but may still note the frequent calls.

Not calling often enough

Calling once a month or so is on the other end of the range.

Part of what puts luck on our side is persistence, but longer timeframes like that often reduce the positive impact. There's a similar problem when leaving messages—prospects may not hear your message often enough for repetition to have an effect.

Three popular frequencies

If daily is probably too often and monthly may be too infrequent, what's just right? There are three frequencies that work well for many callers. As you read about these, notice how frequency ties in with putting schedules in the calendar.

Twice a week:

Many callers report good results from calling twice a week. These callers tend to focus on calling, and have fewer other tasks on their plates. If you look at their calendar, you'll see two or more full days each and every week devoted to preparing, calling, and following through.

Weekly:

Another popular frequency is calling weekly—but not exactly every seven days. Using a number other than seven helps alter the day of the week almost automatically. For example: If you call on Wednesday, you'll next call prospects on Thursday and then Friday, and so on. Using six or five days does the same thing.

When using this approach: most callers move their calling schedule along with the next calling day. (If they call on a Wednesday the next week's call session is on Thursday.)

A wide range of callers find weekly frequency works well. Their calendars show time blocked for preparation, calling and follow through at least once a week.

Every two weeks:

The third popular frequency is calling every two weeks or so. Again, the number of days is not exactly 14, so the days of the week change over time.

This frequency works well for people who have many other tasks to handle, including demos and longer sales conversations with prospects (which should occur separately).

How this is scheduled varies quite a bit. Some reps' calendars show one to two-hour blocks sprinkled throughout their week, others spend a full day.

Tips about Frequency

No matter which frequency you consider for your calling system, make sure to consider the rest of your schedule, too. If you won't be able to fit calling in once a week, do not use a weekly frequency.

Find and use a frequency that fits. Do not set a higher frequency as some sort of stretch goal because stretch goals do not work.

Frequency and prospect-categories

Some people categorize prospects based on things like potential account value. Here are tips for this situation:

- Do not vary frequency per category unless you have several hundred or more prospects in each category. If you have fewer than that, use the same frequency for all of them.

- If you do indeed have a large number of prospects in each category (several hundred and more) and want to vary frequency, set and use the same frequency for all prospects within a category.

How many calls or attempts

How frequently you call prospects goes hand-in-hand with how many times you'll try to reach them.

- This element of your system is simple, too: Choose a number of three or greater.

The most popular choice for number of tries is five, however, many callers use more. You can almost pick a number out of the air, as long as it's at least three.

The System (so far)

Your system includes frequency: how often to call. Let's say you decide to call prospects every nine days (give or take weekends, holidays, etc.).

Persistence will pay off, but you also need to have room to focus on opportunities—so your system also includes a number of attempts.

Let's say you choose five attempts (the most common choice). Is that really enough tries to help put luck on your side? No, it's not; which is why your system also covers what happens after that "last" try.

What Happens Next

OUR EXAMPLE SYSTEM: Call prospects every nine days (frequency), and try to reach them five times. So far, so good. However, we need to continue to market to prospects in order to put luck on our side and that's what the "Next" part of the system covers.

The idea is to continue reaching out, but less often and/or with other marketing tools—putting these prospects on a back burner to simmer.

Option for Next: Call less and less often

One option for the "Next" in your system is to continue to call these prospects, but less often. For example:

- If your system starts with calling every two weeks, you might drop that to every three weeks or monthly (monthly is fine for this part of your system).

- Make sure to choose the number of tries for this "next" frequency, too. (Use at least three attempts).

Example

- Julia's system starts with calling prospects every nine days, and she makes five attempts.

- What happens next with prospects she has not yet reached: Julia calls them every three weeks, and makes three attempts.

- What happens next with prospects she has not yet reached: Frequency drops to every five weeks. There's no maximum number of tries for this tier of her system, she just keeps calling.

Julia has a total of three tiers in her system. The first two have a frequency and a maximum number of attempts. The third and last tier maintains marketing efforts—it has a frequency but no maximum number of attempts.

Option for Next: Mail or email

Another popular option is to use mail and/or email. This includes mailing or emailing articles or "newsletters," as well as contacting prospects via social media.

If you choose this option, be sure to define how often you'll mail or email prospects (frequency), and how many times you'll do that. The minimum number of tries is still three.

Some people have more than one tier for mail and/or email, too, setting frequency and number of attempts for each tier.

Spotlight on using email

Because email takes less effort in some ways, many people use this marketing tool for the "Next" in the system. Most set a frequency but do not have a maximum number of attempts or tiers—they simply use email over the long term.

Example

- Kevin's system starts with calling prospects every six days. He makes six attempts.

- Next for prospects he has not reached: Kevin emails something to them monthly (articles, product highlights, letters, etc.).There is no maximum number of attempts.

Option for Next: Mix and match

Many people alternate calling and mail/email. Here's an example:

- Call prospects weekly. Try six times.

- Next: email every two weeks. Try three times.

- Next: call weekly. Try three times.

- Next: email monthly. (No maximum number of times.)

That's just an example and your system may be different. The important thing is to define a system and apply it.

System Summary (so far)

- Frequency: How often will you call prospects?

- Maximum attempts: How many times you will try to reach prospects? (Use a minimum of three.)

- What happens next: How will you continue to market to these prospects?

Does your "Next" have tiers? If so, what marketing tools will you use, how often, and how many tries for each tier?

Using a systematic approach supports success with less effort. The same is true for the elements which may vary more often: which time and day to call.

When to Call

PEOPLE OFTEN ASK whether there is a good day of the week or time of day to call. Continual analysis over a few decades with thousands of callers and a wide variety of industries provides this general answer: they're all good.

However, you may find some days and times are better—or worse—for yourself and your market. Before we jump into details, here's a mini lecture about completing your own analysis.

Best vs. not so good

When analyzing data; sometimes what jumps out is clearly better than the rest, and sometimes what jumps out is clearly not as good.

The same thing applies to personal preference. Sometimes we know what we like right away, sometimes we're immediately clear on what we do not like.

Either of those (best or not so good) are valid factors to use in your system. For example, if you know what day of the week you *do not* want to call, don't stress over determining your best day (and don't call on your least favorite day).

Time of day

The best time of day to call is almost always based on your own natural energy.

Do you tend to feel more energized in the morning? Then that's your best time to call. Do you feel more energized and focused in the afternoon? Then that's your best time to call.

Use the less-energized time periods to research, clean up lists, send letters and emails, and so on.

However, you may find your up-period is best for drafting scripts. Experiment to see if this is the case.

All of that said: once you're calling, pay attention to time of day in which you reach more (or fewer) prospects. e.g., If lots of prospects seem to be away from their desk in the morning, it will be better to call in the afternoon.

As for what happens if you cannot make calls during your most energized time, I'll provide tips in a bit.

Tip for calling individuals at home

At least once a year, someone asks for help in reaching prospects they're calling at home. This would not be worth mentioning except for one thing: invariably, they're calling prospects at home when most of those prospects are at work.

Even in this age of highly portable phones, it does not make sense to call people at a home number when they're likely to be at work. What to do instead? Call their work phone.

The other option for reaching people at home: call their home phone in the early evening or on weekends. (Be sure to follow Do Not Call rules, including time limits.)

Day of the week

Though identifying best time of day starts with you, day of the week is often based on your prospects.

Avoid choosing days of the week based on when you think prospects will be most receptive mood-wise (e.g., Friday). Give yourself time to collect actual data, and then choose based on what that data shows.

A not-good day may be more obvious

Day of the week is a factor for which a not-good day often stands out more than a best day.

For example, one of my prospect groups is senior management of community banks. I eventually noticed the contact rates were low on Tuesdays. Their assistants filled me in: Tuesday is a popular day for executive and board meetings, so those bosses are often in meetings most of the day (or scrambling to get ready for them).

Once I knew Tuesday was not a great day to reach these particular prospects, it was easy to adjust and call on other days.

System Summary (yet again), and Next

The system is simple:

- Frequency
- Number of attempts (at least three)
- What happens next?

The system also includes:

- When you'll call (days of the week, and time of day)

Even the most well-planned system won't help if it's not applied, so let's turn to putting your system to work.

Using Your System Over Time

THE WAY TO make a system powerful is to use it systematically. This may prompt a silent "duh," but making time to make calls is where things fall apart for many.

"My schedule changes all the time," people say. "I try to make calls but other things get in the way," is the other common comment.

The key to solving those and similar problems is to make time the same way you make time for work meetings, sales appointments, and so on: by putting it in your calendar.

Schedule in your calendar, in advance

Most people have a somewhat predictable work schedule. We know we've got a weekly meeting or two or three—and they're often in our calendar. Our work schedule usually varies a bit, too. We have every third Monday off because we work every third Saturday, but which Monday changes month to month. We have phone and in-person sales conversations sprinkled here and there. We schedule "out of office" to make sure we can take our kiddo to her Judo tournament. If we're organized, we put these events in our calendar, too.

The same thing applies to calling. Making time to call is often as simple as actually putting it in your calendar. Schedule that ahead and your system has a solid infrastructure.

Use time blocking

Success with cold calling involves more than making the calls themselves. There are three chunks of activities:

- You need time to prepare and perhaps practice scripts, time to prepare your call list, and you may need time to do a bit of research.

- You need time to make the calls.

- You need time to follow through; sending mail and emails, updating CRM, and so on.

Do not prepare a script, make a call, update the CRM, refresh the script, make another call, update the CRM... This back-and-forth won't let you get into the swing of calling and your calls won't be as successful. The best practice is to use blocks of time—one hour or more—for each type of task. This means your calendar should have time separately blocked for:

- Preparation
- Calling
- Follow through

Scheduling tips

Do not schedule time day-by-day; schedule ahead for the upcoming week or two weeks (or month or more). Be sure to schedule ahead based on what's most predictable for yourself, whether that's the next week or several months.

Block time in your calendar to set the upcoming schedule. For example, people with highly variable schedules often find Friday is a perfect day to firm-up plans for the upcoming week. Their calendars show a block of time for "plan next week" on each and every Friday.

You may find showing "calling session" in your calendar helps protect that time from interruptions. However, only show "calling" or "calling session" for the block of time in which you're making calls, not for preparation or follow through. (If you show "calling" for all of those things, people will expect results commensurate with that total time.)

There's no benefit in scheduling calling right after preparation. In fact, they're such different tasks it's often helpful to put them far apart.

However, there are benefits in scheduling follow-through time right after the block of time devoted to calling. Fresher memory helps us note more information without having to break from calling to do that.

Remember to schedule calling time when you are generally most energetic. This doesn't mean you need to feel bubbly, just more focused and energetic.

Treat calling sessions as important appointments—do not cancel them even for sales conversations. If you make a habit of canceling calling sessions for "better" things, you'll soon find your pipeline is drying up.

I want to re-emphasize this point: block a separate time for preparation, a separate time for calling, and a separate time for follow through.

Blocking a separate time for making calls is particularly important because making many calls in a row helps you get into the swing of it. Callers who give themselves the freedom to focus enjoy far better results.

Making changes to your system

As you start to use your system, do not give in to the temptations to analyze it daily or change it often. These temptations are usually more about procrastination and what the old sales dogs call the "paralysis of analysis."

Give your system some time before you evaluate and make changes. Base changes on data, not your gut feeling. (There are tips for gathering and analyzing data in the Managing Your Metrics section.)

Tips for boosting energy

Let me start with a non-tip about standing up while making calls. Some people find this helps them feel energized and focused, just as many experience the opposite effect!

Experiment with standing if you wish, but don't let others boss you around about it. In case this helps, I'm one of those who is more easily distracted when standing, so it doesn't help me.

While we're on the subject of non-tips: posting a mirror, or a picture meant to show what you get when you reach sales goals, does not work well for most people.

Posting pictures or quotes that make you smile or feel good does work well for many; however, again, don't let others boss you around about this. If it works for you, great. If not, don't force it.

Provide your body with real fuel: nutritious food and water (not half a bag of chips and two energy drinks).

Pay attention to how you feel about one hour after lunch. Many people experience an energy dip at that time, which is a bit counterintuitive. If this is true for you, plan to take a break or don't call at all during that time.

By the time we realize we're tired, it's usually too late. Call no longer than 45 to 60 minutes in one sitting. If you have more dials to make, take a short break and come back to calling. If you're really dragging, take very short but more frequent breaks: a five minute break every 30 minutes or so will do wonders.

Another tip for low-energy days is to stand up and sit back down every few dials. If you cannot stand, do something to move your body a bit—even a neck stretch can help.

Some people find it helpful to call from a private area, such as a conference room or your home.

Last but not least: reduce your dials goal so you don't add frustration onto lower energy.

About That "Last" Voicemail

THERE'S ONE LAST thing to cover before we leave the system section, and that is the "last" voicemail.

When we have not reached prospects, it's easy to think they're not paying attention. Many are actually paying attention—they're just not calling back. In fact, many are paying enough attention to notice when we suddenly stop calling.

On our end of the phone line, we're applying a system (e.g., we changed from weekly to monthly calls). On their end of the phone line, we may seem a bit flaky. To avoid a bad impression, your "last" message should let prospects know you'll be making a change.

Example "last" message

Julia's system uses five attempts. Her "last" message:

This is Julia, from Speakers Success Camp. 925 555 1234. I'd like to see if our programs would provide value to your executives. And others who need to make the most of formal presentations.

I see in my notes this is my 5th call. My guess is this is not at the top of your to-do list right now. I'll be in touch, but less often. Feel free to call me. Julia. 925 555 1234.

About that example

The first part of the voicemail follows the standard format: Who You Are, Phone Number, Why You're Calling.

The second part acknowledges there have been a few messages (five). It also puts possible low interest on the table with "not at the top of your to-do list". This statement helps Julia sound confident and professional, yet keeps the door open for things to change.

The second part of the message also says what Julia plans to do next: call less often. However, it does not give a specific timetable for that; in fact, it doesn't say how she'll be in touch.

TIP: Do not tell prospects exactly what you plan to do. This gives you flexibility, and makes follow through easier to manage.

Also notice there is no call to action in this message; instead, Julia invites prospects to call her. The reason for that is it's hard to say, "I guess you're not interested" and "call me back" in the same message. We end up sounding peevish or demanding or just plain awkward.

Another example

This is Julia, from Speakers Success Camp. 925 555 1234. I'd like to see if our programs would provide value to your executives. And others who need to make the most of formal presentations.

I see in my notes I've reached out a number of times. Looks like this may not be of high interest right now. I'll continue to give you a call from time to time. Feel free to call me. Julia. 925 555 1234.

One more example

Julia uses a few tiers in her system. For the last tier, Julia switches from calling to mailing. Here's the message she leaves as she makes that change:

This is Julia. Speakers Success Camp. 925 555 1234. Our programs teach executives and sales reps how to make the most of formal presentations. I'd like to see if they'd be a good fit for your company.

I plan to send you case studies and other materials. And hope you'll keep your eye open for them. Of course, I'd be happy to discuss a potential fit, as well. Julia. 925 555 1234.

Julia's message does not specifically say she will no longer be calling, just that she plans to mail stuff now. This makes it easy for her to call if she wishes.

Why an open approach works best

Every few years, a supposedly new way to use mail, email or voicemail comes onto the scene. This "new" approach involves telling prospects we're going to call or mail them in a specific number of days, and then we're supposed to do that. The premise is we catch prospects' attention by actually doing what we say we will.

One problem with that is reliance on prospects reading the letters and caring about our plan. The other major problem is on our end—something gets in the way and we do not do as promised. Using an open approach hides any lack of follow-through and does no harm.

Open messages also allow us to react to changes in our market and situation. Maybe we call more often than planned because our services meet a need that's suddenly in the news. Maybe we get so busy we won't be calling for a while (we can mail or email, instead). Maybe our new boss says we may only mail or email using opt-in (so we go back to calling). Maybe we don't feel like managing a complex system.

In short: open messages avoid common errors and streamline things for us.

Two final points about "last" messages

The reason there are quotes around "last" voicemail message is because we rarely stop marketing to prospects altogether.

However, sometimes there are long stretches between calls and messages to some prospects. When this happens, there's no need to explain why there was a long stretch but you may want to acknowledge the gap in some way.

This is Julia. Speakers Success Camp. 925 555 1234. Our programs teach executives and sales reps how to make the most of formal presentations.

It's been a while since I reached out to you. I'd like to see if our programs would provide value to your company. Please give me a call. Julia. 925 555 1234.

Notice that message includes a call to action. That's because it's best to start over in these cases, applying your strategy from step one.

The last point I need to make about your strategy is that you should stop if prospects tell you to stop calling, emailing, etc.

Whether calling B2B or B2C, you're required to maintain an internal Do Not Call and Do Not Mail list.

Do not make them say the exact magic words to be added to the list, either. Someone who doesn't want to hear from you is not a good challenge, they are NAP—Not a Prospect.

Voicemail, creating and using a system...
That's mostly about dealing with prospects we did not reach

Time to cover what happens when you reach prospects
but they're not ready for a next step sales conversation

FOLLOWING THROUGH

Staying in Touch

What to Say Next Time

Rating Prospects

We are confronted with insurmountable opportunities.

(Pogo – the cartoon character, that is)

Staying in Touch

LET'S GO BACK to the point when you ask prospects for a next step—a sales conversation. It may look like these examples:

I'd like to explore the fit. Are you open to that?

Can we set up a meeting?

Shall we see if our services would provide value to your company?

There will be times when prospects agree to that next step and on you go. There will also be times when prospects do not agree to take a next step. What happens then?

Not now is not an objection

If the prospect has an objection to meeting, see if you can handle that objection. However, it's important to know "not now" is not an objection. If you try to push prospects to move forward before they're ready, most will push right back. Even if you succeed in pushing them to move forward, things are likely to fall apart down the road.

When prospects are not open to having a sales conversation at this time, do not treat that as an objection. However, you can still use the call-back strategy—in fact, it's perfect for this situation.

Use the Call-back Strategy

Here's a review of the strategy.

- Step 1: Ask if you can call back down the road.

- Optional Step 2: If the prospect says you may: ask for a general time frame to call again.

- Optional Step 3: If the time frame sounds somewhat specific, see if there's a reason behind that.

Though steps 2 and 3 are still optional, using all three steps (when appropriate) helps build relationships in "not now" situations.

Example

You're an insurance broker. You ask for the next step and the prospect says, "We may be open to talking with new brokers, but not at this time."

You reply, *"Fair enough. Mind if I check back with you?"*

Prospect says sure. You say, *"What kind of timing would be appropriate?"*

Prospect tells you, "Five weeks."

You know when their renewal dates are and 'five weeks' doesn't seem to connect. So you say, *"Will do. I'm a bit curious about that timeframe. Anything going on between now and then?"*

Prospect says, "We may be acquiring a competitor and risk will be part of overall assessment. An outside perspective may be valuable."

That's good to know! You make a quick note, close the call, finish the rest of your calls, and then update CRM with the information and next-call date.

Example

You sell printing services. When you ask for the next step, the prospect tells you they will have some major print needs in the near future but he's too busy to meet right now.

You try to stay cool (good idea) so you calmly say, *"I definitely want to have an opportunity to earn your business. When's a good time to check back with you about meeting?"*

Prospect says, "After the 17th of this month."

Since that's not far away, you decide not to ask why (another good idea) and close the call.

You make a quick note for this prospect, finish the rest of your calls, and then update CRM with the next-call date.

Example

You're a banker. When you ask for the next step the prospect says, "We just changed our banking relationship but, frankly, we're not happy. However, I want to give it some time."

You reply, *"That's certainly reasonable. I'd like to stay in touch in a couple ways. I'd like to email articles you may find of interest. And I'd like to check in with you by phone. May I?"*

Prospect says sure. You get his email and then ask, "As much as I want opportunity to earn your business, I want to respect your timing. What's a general time frame for giving you a call?"

Prospect says, "Call me June 12."

You think that sounds pretty specific so you say, *"That sounds pretty specific. May I know what's behind that time frame?"*

Prospect tells you, "That's a deadline. It will be six months to the day and that's plenty of time for them to get their act together. Or not."

Again, good to know. You close the call, make a quick note, finish the rest of your calls, and then update CRM with the information and next-call date.

Example

You are you. After you ask for the next step the prospect says, "This sounds interesting but I'm not open to meeting at this time, not even informationally."

You reply, *"Fair enough. I'd like to stay in touch. Sound good to you?"*

Prospect says that would be fine. You say, *"I'd like to use a timeline that makes sense for you. What would that be?"*

Prospect replies, "Oh, I don't know. Any time."

You suggest, *"How about next month?"*

Prospect again says that's fine, you close the call, make a note for the prospect, finish the rest of your calls, and then update CRM with the next-call date.

Making notes versus updating CRM

You may have spotted a trend in the above examples about making a note but updating the CRM later.

You'll have the most success if you make calls in a row. If you update CRM after each call, you'll lose that flow and momentum.

But you still need to make notes, right? The solution is to make abbreviated notes while calling—often on paper—and update CRM after all calls are finished.

I highly recommend spiral notebooks because they're inexpensive, easy to use, and store old notes in one spot. (I keep them for one year, remove any sheets with notes I want to keep, pull out the spiral part and toss rest into a recycle bin.)

What to Say Next Time

WE JUST LOOKED at what to do when you reach prospects but they're not ready to schedule a sales conversation. Now, let's look at what happens the next time you call.

Let's begin with a reality check: even when prospects give you a specific timeframe to call again, that does not necessarily indicate they're a "hotter" prospect.

In fact, many prospects will suggest a new timeframe again and again, each time you call. Try not to let that get you down. Remember, staying in touch puts luck on your side— so do it!

The above reality also means creating a script for every single prospect won't be worth it, and may instead generate frustration. You need a script that works for *most* prospects, whether it's your second or fifth call to each of them.

That script should also make it easy to mention prior calls. However, be careful not to make it sound as if they made some sort of promise or an appointment. Here's an example of what to avoid:

"This is Shawn. I'm with Savage and Greene, the sales training company. When we spoke last month, you told me I should call at this time. How much time do you have to discuss our programs and your training needs?"

This works much better:

This is Shawn. I'm with Savage and Greene, a sales training company. We'd like to see if our programs would provide value to your organization. You might remember we spoke a while ago. You suggested I try again around this time. I'd like to set a phone appointment to explore a possible fit. Are you open to doing that?

The wording doesn't even assume the prospect will remember the prior call. The part where the script mentions the last time you spoke is also very general, so it will work for most situations.

All of the above said, there will be situations in which you want to have a more prospect-specific script.

More prospect-specific

Sometimes prospects will have mentioned something you want to fold into the script for the current call. When you do this, try to keep your expectations low and your wording general. Let me illustrate why this is a good guideline.

In one of the earlier examples, a prospect explained the timeframe he gave relates to a deadline for the new bank to perform up to snuff.

When the banker calls again she says, "This is Devon, with XYZ Bank. Last time we spoke, you mentioned your new bank was not providing satisfactory service. And suggested I call at this time. How is their service at this point?"

Prospect says, "I don't remember saying that. In any case, we're happy with our bank."

Drat. What happened? What happened is the banker's call was just a few minutes out of the prospect's day, week, month, and quarter. Things have moved on in the meantime.

In addition, the banker read into what the prospect said. "Not happy" didn't have to be about service; it could have been about products or features, locations, fees or credit terms (and more). Her script for her next call dug a hole that's hard to escape.

Examples

Here's an example of how to more safely mention what the prospect said the last time you spoke:

This is Devon, with XYZ Bank. I'd like the opportunity to earn your business. Last time we spoke, you mentioned you had a new bank and suggested I check in at this time.

Your current relationship may be satisfactory. Nonetheless, I'd like the chance to see if our services and products may be of value, too. Can we set up a meeting?

Notice that example skipped the part about the prospect being unhappy with the new bank. This prevents the caller from sounding assumptive, and reminds her brain to have reasonable expectations.

Also notice almost all of the script looks exactly like scripts covered before, including using a technique to help prevent a common objection ("we're happy with our bank"). General scripting practices do apply!

A prospect told the printer's rep they'd have some major print needs in the near future and suggested he call again on the 17th. Here's the printer's script for this call:

This is Justin. I'm with Print World. We spoke just a couple weeks ago. You mentioned you may have some print needs coming up and suggested I call at this time. I'd love the opportunity to explore the business fit. Can we set up a meeting to do that?

Another prospect suggested the printer's rep call next month, with no particular reason given. Here's what Justin prepared and used:

This is Justin. I'm with Print World. We spoke briefly about a month ago. I'd love the opportunity to see if our services would help your company's materials shine. Can we set up a meeting to explore a fit?

That example barely mentions the prior call—just enough to provide context without digging any holes.

TIP: Scripting for prospect-specific calls

You might recall one best practice is to create general scripts, not one script per prospect. This applies to these calls; however, you may also want to mention the last call—which is probably different for each prospect.

One way to deal with this scripting challenge is to leave a spot open for mentioning what the prospect said last time. Do not show something like "(Mention last call)" because that will actually require your brain to work harder. Just leave an open or blank space as a reminder to glance at the notes for each prospect and say something that fits.

Another way to deal with this challenge is to type your script using bullet-points, not full sentences. The script might look like this:

- Justin. With Print World.
- Spoke
- Love opportunity to see if services would help company shine
- Can we set up a meeting?

As with the first option, you'll glance at your notes for each prospect and mention the last conversation at the "Spoke" point.

Many callers find either of the above work well. However, if neither of those work for you, go ahead and create a script for each prospect.

Nonspecific script example

I just covered the situation in which we have something specific to mention to prospects (something from our last call).

However, it's just as common that we will call and do not have anything in particular to mention—the prospects didn't share any information, didn't do anything more than give us the go-ahead to call again, and so on. It's still important to create a script for these calls. Here's what it may look like:

This is Justin, with Print World. I'd love the opportunity to see if our services would help your company's materials shine. I'm checking in to see if we can set up a meeting to explore a fit. Are you open to scheduling one?

The phrase "I'm checking in" provides a context or reminder without digging a hole for the caller.

Again: Don't let a number get you down

As we follow through, we may call some prospects just once before things move on to a sales conversation, and we may call some prospects many times over an extended period. Most situations fall somewhere in the middle of the range.

Do not focus on the number of times you've called a prospect, or for how long you've been trying. Instead, remember how you put luck on your side: by giving yourself lots of opportunities to reach the right people at the right time. Persistence will pay off.

Key Points, and Next

Luck and timing affect cold calling. Some prospects will be interested and ready to take the next step after our first call, many will not. One of the ways we put luck on our side is to call those prospects again.

It is counter-productive (and unrealistic) to create a separate script for each prospect as we call the second time, third time, and so on.

We don't want to wing it with these calls, either. The solution is to create general scripts that also have space to mention something specific, when applicable.

Now...many callers want to apply a rating to these prospects. If I were the boss of your decision I'd say skip it—not worth the effort. Those of you who are not magically persuaded by that statement should go ahead and read the next chapter.

Rating Prospects

THERE ARE MANY ways to rate prospects. The majority of them do not work for one simple reason: when cold calling, we do not yet have enough information about prospects—which makes rating them a guess.

Once we have had at least one actual <u>sales</u> conversation, we have good information to rate prospects. You can find articles on rating these prospects in the Selling section of the Savage and Greene blog.

Good reasons not to rate

Before you have had at least one sales conversation, trying to rate prospects can be a waste of time.

Rating these prospects can also make you think you know more about them than you do. This leads to unrealistic expectations, which leads to frustration.

Trying to rate prospects also clutters up your CRM with useless data points, which may in turn clutter up your and your manager's time with useless discussion.

For all those reasons, I encourage you not to rate prospects at this point. But if you really, really want to rate them, a system is shown below.

Maintain the line

If you rate these prospects, it's still important to maintain that line between prospecting/marketing, and selling.

You'll need one type of rating for your sales pipeline (prospects with which you have had at least one actual sales conversation), and another type of rating for the rest.

Since I recommend points (a number) for rating prospects in the sales pipeline, the prospecting rating system shown on the next page uses letters.

Rating: If you <u>are not</u> qualifying prospects

- Prospects with whom you have not yet connected:

  Identify them with a zero or leave this blank. If you've left them messages, and they called you back but you have not spoken with them, that's still a zero or blank.

- Prospects with whom you have actually connected:

  Identify them with an "A."

- For prospects with whom you've connected *and a sales conversation has been scheduled:*

  Identify these with a "B."

  If the appointment for the sales conversation was not kept and no new appointment is scheduled: Take the rating back to A. Do this whether the prospect politely canceled or not, and even if it was you who had to cancel. If there's no sales conversation actually scheduled, it's an A.

Rating: If you <u>are</u> qualifying prospects

Qualifying adds a layer to calls, which means the rating system needs another letter.

- Prospects with whom you have not yet connected:

  Identify them with a zero or leave this blank. (If you've left them messages, and they called you back but you have not spoken with them, that's still a zero or blank.)

- Prospects with whom you have actually connected:

  Identify them with an "A."

- If you have connected <u>and</u> you were able to confirm they qualify:

  Identify these prospects with a "B."

- For qualified prospects with whom you've connected *and a sales conversation has been scheduled:*

  Identify these with a "C."

  If the appointment for the sales conversation was not kept and no new appointment is scheduled: Take the rating back to B. Do this whether the prospect politely canceled or not, and even if it was you who had to cancel. If there's no sales conversation actually scheduled, it's an B.

About rating and qualifying

Some callers find the added letter in the rating system that includes qualifying doesn't fit very well. Choosing the rating feels complicated, different reps and their managers don't agree on the right rating, or rating takes too much time.

Those are actually clues qualifying doesn't fit. If this happens to you, skip qualifying as an experiment to see if you really need it.

Next

It is not a good idea to count calls to each prospect, but it is a good idea to set goals for number of calls in general. Time to cover metrics, including setting and using dials goals.

MANAGING YOUR METRICS

The Beauty of Dials Goals

How to Set and Use Dials Goals

Another Secret Weapon

It's my understanding that there would be no math.

(Chevy Chase, playing presidential candidate Gerald Ford)

The Beauty of Dials Goals

WHETHER YOU'RE HIGHLY goal-oriented or not, when you pick up the phone you probably have some sort of objective in mind.

Your objective should not be to sell a certain amount. That pulls your focus too far away, and tends to encourage an ineffective approach.

Your goal should not be to set a certain number of sales meetings, or even to reach a certain number of prospects. The first is assumptive, the second ignores the part luck and timing play.

You'll have the greatest success if you try to control only the stuff you really <u>can</u> control:

- Making the calls
- Saying what you want to say
- Responding to what prospects say and do

That's all you need to control to enjoy great success! And since what you control begins with making calls, that's the goal you should set—how many calls to make—also known as "dials" goals.

Dials goals: a simple tool for powerful focus

When we think about the overall process, we understand making calls generates sales conversations, which generate new business. However, that understanding is actually too broad to help us focus. We need something more...well, focused.

Dials goals give us something distinct on which to concentrate—again, the thing that starts the whole ball rolling.

Dials goals: adding a missing marker of success

Another thing that supports great success is the ability to know you are doing what you need to do.

Setting dials goals adds an important marker to the markers of appointments and sales. And reaching the dials goal tells us we're doing what's needed to succeed.

How to Set Dials Goals

I'M GOING TO cover three ways to set dials goals (and one we can no longer use). One method works especially well if feeling anxious while in the learning curve, so let's begin with that one.

Setting dials goals using PFA

PFA stands for "pulled from air." The idea is to set a dials goal based on how you feel. Because this allows your mood to rule, this method works particularly well for those who are anxious and in the learning curve (but can backfire after that).

It's simple: choose a dials goal you feel or think you can hit in <u>one</u> sitting. As you go through the learning curve, increase the dials goal as your skills and comfort level increase.

Example

Bridget feels quite anxious about calling and sets her goal at five dials.

She blocks two hours per week to cover preparation, calling, and follow through. Bridget enters this schedule in her calendar for the next four weeks.

As she calls, Bridget finds she doesn't need nearly that amount of time for five dials and preparation and follow through. And each time she makes calls, hits her dials goal, builds skills—and nothing horrible occurs—she feels more comfortable.

She increases her dials goal for the third week, and again for the fourth week. After that, Bridget feels ready to set dials goals another way.

Tips for PFA

Using dials goals helps us focus. Hitting the goal reminds us we're doing something important: giving ourselves lots of opportunities to reach enough people, to have enough sales conversations, to have enough new business. Stretch goals completely undermine the positive effect, so do not set them. Set goals you can hit.

If you're feeling especially nervous or anxious, set a dials goal as low as Bridget's five dials. However, don't go below that because you need some repetitions for skills and experience to sink in.

Do not use PFA goals on a long-term basis. If you still feel you need them after a month or so, contact me for some help.

See the chapter on getting through the learning curve for more tips.

Setting dials goals using time

This method works very well for most callers, including people who need to add calling into an existing schedule. The key is to use a reasonable guideline for number of calls per hour: **25 to 30**.

That guideline covers most callers. If your calls tend to be on the shorter side, you may be able to adjust up from 30 per hour. If your calls tend to be longer, you may not be able to make 25 dials in one hour and should adjust the goal downward.

Choose number of hours and multiply

The number of hours may be per month, per week, or per day—match this choice to your approach to scheduling. Callers often have trouble visualizing how this works, so here are some examples:

- Maria blocks time weekly, scheduling a full day for calling and other marketing tasks.

  Maria's full day covers preparation, calling, follow through and things such as adding to the company blog. *Within that day*, she blocks two hours back-to-back for calling, and her dials goal is 60.

- Sawyer also blocks time on a weekly basis. He starts with *three hours of calling per week* and a weekly dials goal of 75.

  Sawyer's schedule varies from week to week. Some weeks, he has one-hour calling sessions on Monday, Wednesday and Friday and uses a dials goal of 25 for each. Some weeks, he schedules two hours of calling on one day (dials goal of 50), and one hour on another day (dials goal is 25).

  Sawyer also schedules and blocks time for preparation and follow through; adding a couple hours for the week. Though he has a weekly dials goal, it's important to note he also uses a dials goal for <u>each</u> calling session, which ensures getting full benefit from those goals.

- Brenden starts with a monthly dials goal of 250. Using 25 dials per hour, he blocks time throughout the month.

  The details of Brenden's calling schedule change from month to month; however, he usually schedules calling every two weeks so he can stay in touch with prospects on a timely basis.

  Brenden doesn't just block time for calling, he also blocks time for preparation and follow through.

  Though he sets a monthly dials goal, Brenden also has a dials goal for each calling session—using the guideline of 25 dials per hour as his goal—so he benefits each time and stays on track to succeed.

Tips for goals using time

The above are common examples meant to help you get started. Use the tips shown below, and some experimentation, to figure out what works for you.

Use the guideline of 25 to 30 dials per hour as a guideline to start.

Set goals you can reasonably hit. Do not use stretch goals because this de-motivates most people.

Remember to block time so you can make calls all in a row, i.e., one hour is blocked just for calling; not for preparation, calling, and follow through.

Make as many calls in a row as you can. However, be sure to take a break every 45 minutes or so and call no longer than 60 minutes at one sitting. (By the time you realize you need a break, it's usually too late.)

If you discover you often have ten or fewer dials to make after taking a break, reduce your dials goal. It's more effective to use your time and energy well, as opposed to pushing for a certain goal.

Do not divide the guideline (25 to 30 dials per hour) into small bits of time, such as 15 minutes. Sure, we can do the math, but something gets lost in the process. Either make more time for calling, or use the next method for setting dials goals.

Dials goals based on a stack

As mentioned, setting a dials goal gives us something to focus on, and reaching that goal gives us an important marker of success. Setting a number as a goal works well, using a physical stack of paper or index cards works well, too.

Instead of using a list on paper or in CRM, put prospect/contact information on large index cards or separate sheets of paper (one prospect per card or sheet).

Choose a stack of cards or sheets: this stack represents your goal.

Call one-by-one, making a very brief note of date, whether you left a message or spoke with the prospect, next time you'll call, etc. (e.g., 10/22/16: VM Next 10/27)

After each call, put the card or sheet to one side or turn it over. Continue until you've called the entire stack.

Place cards or sheets in a tickler file as applicable (so you know when to call again). That's it!

Tips

If you're feeling frustrated by the calling process, this method may be just what you need. Using something you can touch often helps the sense of accomplishment sink in.

This method also works very well for people who tend to mail or email, and then call. Using paper email and letter copies gives you a handy way to manage overall marketing for each prospect.

This method also works well for people who do not have a high number of prospects to call. Using paper adds heft, making it easier to know you've accomplished what you need to at this point.

Be sure to use something that has enough room to make notes.

Do not choose a stack larger than you can call in one session.

An old method we can no longer use

Back when I was a sales pup, we used an equation to set expectations and identify benchmarks for performance. The equation started at the top of the proverbial funnel with calling, flowed through several points—contact, appointments, qualifying, asking for the business—down to the small end of the funnel and new business.

We used the same equation in reverse to set dials goals based on desired units of new business.

Unfortunately, the data needed to fully feed that equation has not been gathered for quite a while. We have good data for the top of the funnel (dials and contact/response rates). But we have nothing from there, which makes using the full equation a questionable practice.

In prior editions of this book, I'd explain all of the above, share the equation, and add a bunch of cautions about using it to set dials goals. In fact, I had written the latest version for this edition when it struck me...there's no way to do that without also misleading readers.

Instead, I'll say that if someone suggests using a calculation that begins with units of new business and multiplies "up" the funnel to set dials goals, run screaming away. Without good data to feed the equation at each point, the calculation becomes a fancy WAG (wild guess).

Tips for <u>using</u> dials goals

Here are general tips for avoiding common errors with using dials goals. Some may look familiar (they bear repeating).

Which dials count?

All of them count. They all count statistically, they all count realistically—and they all count toward helping you focus and succeed with cold calling.

Each call counts as one dial/one call.

Each call counts as one if it's your first call to a prospect, the second call, the third or sixty-third call. This includes calls to existing customers, networking contacts, people you're referred to, prospects, etc.

Each call counts as one dial when a human answers (whether it's your contact or not), and when you get voicemail. Each counts as one whether the human listened to you or not.

You should also count wrong numbers, fax screeches, disconnected numbers, bad connections, and language barriers. Each counts as one dial.

Do not parse your calls. They all count, and each call counts as one dial.

Dials goals should fit in one calling session

Every calling session should have its own dials goal. For example:

- Brenden has a monthly dials goal of 250. He schedules calling sessions throughout the month.

- Each calling session has its own dials goal of 50 (with a monthly grand total of 250).

Different scripts may have different dials goals

You may often make calls to different prospects during the same calling session. When the scripts you use are different, you may also want to use different dials goals. Here are some examples:

- Keisha is a banker. In one calling session lasting three hours (including breaks), she plans to call 50 existing consumer-type-customers to market additional services and products to them, and 40 local business owners to market the bank's business services.

  Keisha has created two different scripts: one for customers, and one for business owners.

  She sets separate dials goals: 50 for the calls to customers, and 40 for the calls to business owners.

- Richard wants to invite people to a seminar he's holding. He has 32 clients to call, and 28 prospects to call.

  Richard will use the same script for both groups (he may chat a bit more with clients, but that's not scripted). Since it's the same script, he sets one dials goal of 60.

Make calls in a row

Making a number of calls using the same script gets us into the swing of it and we tend to have better results.

When you're calling different types of prospects in the same calling session, call one group at a time. For example:

- Keisha has customers to call and the script covers consumer-oriented topics. She should make these calls in a row.

  Keisha also has business owners to call and this script covers business-oriented topics. She should make these calls in a row.

- Richard is using one script. He has clients to call. He should make these calls in a row. He also has prospects to call, he should make these calls in a row.

Guidelines again

Thousands of callers have shared their before-training and after-training stats with me, sometimes continuing to update me years after we first met in training.

- That is what informs a reasonable per hour dials guideline:

  25 to 30 dials per hour.

- That's also what continues to validate the response rate:

  25% to 33%.

The above guidelines are good to start with, but identifying your own guidelines will be even better. The tool for doing that—the tracking sheet—does more than clarify your metrics...a lot more.

Tracking Sheet: Another Secret Weapon

THE TRACKING SHEET described in this chapter provides users with strong benefits.

Using it provides a deeper sense of making progress. This can be important when the ultimate pay-off (sales) is far away, and even more important when in the learning curve.

Using the tracking sheet also gives us a way to spot our best (or not so good) days and times to call. Using the sheet also gives us a way to identify our own metrics—the numbers to which "it's a numbers game" refers.

Using the tracking sheet helps us double-check our objectives, and adjust as needed to prevent problems. It places dials goals front and center, so we're more likely to leverage their benefits, too.

Last but not least, the tracking sheet synthesizes a number of best practices into one simple reference, making it easy to apply them.

Write me to get a tracking sheet

It's easier to understand how to use the tracking sheet if you have one in front of you. There's a copy at the back of this book, and this chapter provides an overview. Contact me via savageandgreene.com to get a full-size copy and instructions so you have your own secret weapon.

Data and best practices at the top

Though this is an overview, I'll walk through the tracking sheet bit by bit. At the top are the following fields:

Name

This is a spot in which to write your name. There's no reason to complete this if you're the only one tracking calls and analyzing the data.

Date

Use one tracking sheet per calling session/dials goal. Entering the date will help you organize enough tracking sheets for valid data analysis.

Day of the week

Indicate Monday, Tuesday, Wednesday, etc. You'll need this information to spot good or not-so-good days of the week.

Time of day

This also helps you spot good or not-so-good time periods for calling. Some people show a specific timeframe (e.g., 10 AM to 11:30 AM), others show morning or afternoon. Use just one method and be consistent.

List/prospect type

There are two ways this field can be used:

- If you're using certain lists (whether you built them or purchased them), noting which list was used can clarify whether some sources have better data.

- You can also use this space to note the type of prospect you're calling (e.g., clients, prospects, networking contacts, CEOs, office managers, specific industry). This data can clarify whether there are better results with certain types.

That said, there's no need to make a note in this space if the data won't be used. For example: Would it help to see if more networking contacts take next steps compared to other prospects...or would you continue doing a lot of networking regardless? (After all, there are other reasons to network.) If you'd continue to network, collecting this data has less value.

Objective

There's a space to write your objective for calls. Physically writing it down affects your mindset, and gives you a chance to adjust before you begin calling. For example, "get appointments" sets unrealistic expectations. Adjusting that to "request appointments" puts your mindset and calls on the right path.

When you have more than one objective for a calling session, use separate tracking sheets. For example:

- If you're making calls to *identify* contacts/prospects, and you're also making calls *to* contact/prospects, use two tracking sheets (one for each).

- If you're calling clients and prospects to invite them to a seminar, that's just one objective and you should use one tracking sheet.

Dials goal

Write your dials goal for the calling session in this spot. This is the number of dials you'll make in one sitting, though you may take some brief breaks.

Physically writing it down helps it sink in. Seeing it also gives you a chance to reality-check that goal. Will it probably fit within the time block? Is it realistic?

DO NOT use stretch goals. Do not use a range, either (e.g., 10 to 15).

Reward

Note how you'll reward yourself in this spot. (I'll tell you more about using rewards in the next chapter.) This, too, organizes your thinking and helps ensure you apply a best practice.

Five columns for tracking dials data

In the middle of the tracking sheet are five columns. Each column has a heading, and digits 1 through 60.

The idea is to mark dials off as you call. This tiny physical act has huge positive benefits—it tells your mind *and* body you are indeed doing what you need to do to succeed.

Making a mark in each appropriate column also collects data at the same time. The digits in each column make it easy to analyze this data.

Dials column

This is where you'll mark off each dial. Once you get your tracking sheet, practice making a mark just before or as you dial each number. This builds making a mark into automatic habit.

Remember to count (mark off) all dials, including wrong numbers, faxes, etc.

Voicemail column

The second column is where you mark off every voicemail you reach. Do this even if you are not leaving messages.

There's a spot in this column to note if you're not leaving messages. This allows you to collect data for using both approaches to voicemail.

When you get your sheet, practice making a mark in this column as you get voicemail each time—just as you do for the Dials column—so it becomes an easy habit.

Connect column

If you are making calls to identify contacts/prospects: mark off a digit when you reach a live human and they hear you out. *Do this whether they give you the contact/prospect name or not.*

If you are making calls to contacts/prospects: mark off a digit when you reach that person and they hear you out. *Do this whether they agree to the next step or not.*

Next step column

This column is for marking off each time a contact/prospect agrees to a next step.

When your objective is to request name and contact info for prospects, getting that information is a next step.

When talking with contact/prospects:

- Agreeing that you may try again later is not a next step. Do not make a mark in this column (nor in the NAP column, which I'll explain next).

- Agreeing to receive email or mail is not a next step. Do not make a mark in this column (nor in the NAP column).

- What is a next step? Agreeing to have a sales conversation.

- Agreeing to a demo is a next step ONLY if you made it clear that's also a sales conversation.

NAP column

NAP stands for Not A Prospect. Mark off a digit in this column when you absolutely will not call that number again. This includes disconnected numbers, fax screeches, language barriers, and way-wrong numbers.

NAP also includes prospects who tell you to add their number to your do not call list (see below). It includes prospects who were horribly rude or completely dismissive...unless you plan to try the number again down the road. (Their attitude may change, or the person at that number may change.)

NAP also includes gatekeepers who were horribly rude or completely dismissive...unless you plan to work around them or try the number later. (The person at that number is even more likely to change or have a change in attitude.)

Don't work hard on making these marks an automatic habit because you won't use it nearly as often as the other columns.

A couple points about "Do Not Call"

In addition to using the Do Not Call registry for consumers, callers in the U.S. are required to maintain and abide-by an internal do not call (and email) list.

Individuals and people representing businesses may ask to be added to the list. I believe Canada has similar requirements. Callers in other areas of the world should check local regulations.

Do not try to work around these regulations. Do not wait for prospects or customers to say a specific phrase. Do not differentiate between consumers and businesses. None of this parsing is worth your time—nor worthy of a consultative approach. Just add the names and numbers to your list and do not call again.

Again: Why making marks is a big deal

Marking calls off in applicable columns gathers important data. However, the greatest value comes from physically making those tiny marks.

Marking calls off connects what's going on in your brain with your body—and vice versa. This speeds learning, changes attitude more quickly, and embeds habits at a deeper level.

Notes space

The tracking sheet has space in which to make quick notes. This is not necessarily meant for notes about specific appointments or timeframes to call prospects again. However, you can use it for this if you don't need a lot of space.

Notes space is intended more for more general notes. For example: if the contact information on the list you're using seems to be wrong a lot, you might make a note to look into that.

Focus on the dials goal data

After the calling session, you may be inclined to dive right away into the data collected on the tracking sheet. But there is only one type of data to evaluate each time:

- Did you hit your dials goal? If so, good.

- Want to increase the goal? Go for it!

- If you did not hit the dials goal, consider decreasing it a bit.

  Adjusting the dials goal so it's more reasonable will help build success, whereas continually missing a dials goal will undermine your efforts.

Using the rest of the data

At the end of each calling session, note the total marks on each column, then toss the tracking sheet in a file.

Once you've collected enough tracking sheets to cover over 100 dials (200 or more is much better), it's time to see what the data shows you. Instructions and tips will be included with your tracking sheet.

Tips for using the collected data

I want to repeat this important point: collect a bunch of tracking sheets <u>and then</u> do the math. Do not calculate the tracking sheet percentages after each calling session. Doing that will reinforce a counterproductive short-term perspective, and the calculations aren't likely to be valid anyway.

Instructions for doing the math for each tracking sheet, and the totals, will be included with the tracking sheet. In the meantime, see the next page for a few tips:

If the Connect rate is low

If the connect rate is below 25%, look at each individual tracking sheet. You may be able to spot calling sessions at the lower end without doing the math for each tracking sheet.

If so: look at the days of the week and/or time of day. Is there a trend indicating you should avoid certain days or times?

Just one tracking sheet can throw things off. If there's one with a much lower connect rate, recalculate without it.

If the Connect rate is high

If the connect rate is above 33% that's good, right? Well, sure, but don't get too excited yet. Luck is involved with this, just as it is with a low connect rate.

However, you may be one of those callers who has a clear best day/time for calling! Take a look at individual tracking sheets to see if there is a trend in days of the week and/or times.

Also look for just one tracking sheet with a much higher rate. Recalculate without it to double-check.

About using the Next Step rate

Earlier, I explained we used to be able to use an equation that covered key milestones from calling, all the way to new business. "Next step" (sales conversations) is one of those milestones for which companies no longer collect data. However, you can use the old guideline as long as you do that loosely—very loosely.

Once you have collected 1000 or more Connects, see if your Next Step percentage is around 33%. If it is, that's in line with what used to be the norm. If your Next Step percentage is far lower, you may need to adjust your scripts. Contact me for help.

Dumping myths, effective scripting, preventing and handling objections, best practices, using dials goals and the tracking sheet

What's left?

How to get through the learning curve
and how to use calling over the long term

BUILDING AND ENJOYING SUCCESS

How to Get Through the Learning Curve

Using Calling Whenever You Want

Oh, I just love success!

(Frank N. Furter)

Getting Through the Learning Curve

PEOPLE ARE OFTEN disappointed to hear there will probably be a learning curve.

In a way, that's a compliment to the approach. Things make such good sense that callers feel they'll be comfortable and do well immediately. However, as a trainer, I know most will still need tips for applying the concepts, starting with the hard part.

How a learning curve may feel

Though making consultative style calls may make intuitive sense, actually making calls can feel awkward and uncomfortable. Writing scripts, preparing to handle objections, using the tools and making calls can also feel like hard work. This can be especially dismaying when we expected things to be easier. All of this can also make us wonder if we're doing something wrong.

Feeling awkward and working harder than expected are not signs you're doing things wrong. These are signs you're doing things differently—you're in a learning curve.

Why there's a learning curve

There's a learning curve whenever we do something differently. If we're slightly changing things, the curve tends to be short and easy to handle. If we're changing things significantly, the curve tends to be longer and more challenging.

Don't worry, the learning curve is temporary and the tips in this chapter will help you get through the learning curve. Ah, but wait, there's more to know upfront.

Learning curve with a leap of faith

As we start to apply a new approach or do things differently, feeling uncomfortable and awkward often create doubt, too.

It's common for callers to wonder if they will ever feel more comfortable. Due to the nature of telemarketing, it's even more common to wonder if the approach will work.

There's bound to be time between starting to use consultative calling and seeing sustained positive results. If you had a sales manager pushing you to apply the methods and stick with it, you'd have an outside driver to support you as you take the leap of faith. Many people do not have such a person, so this chapter also tells you how you can do that for yourself.

How habits and actions inform feelings (act as if)

Understanding how our actions affect how we feel can help you deal with—and shorten—the learning curve.

Up until about twenty years ago, it was believed people usually acted a certain way because they felt a certain way. This premise also meant we could essentially think our way into feeling self-confident or comfortable with cold calling (to name two examples).

As the study of neuroscience matured, it became clear the connection tends to work the other way around: our actions strongly affect how we feel. For example, if we act as if we feel confident, we end up truly feeling confident.

What this boils down to is developing cold calling habits—the actions—is what gets us through the learning curve. Developing <u>good</u> habits is also what empowers you to use telemarketing over time, whenever you want to.

You've succeeded with this before

Here's the good news: you've been developing habits and getting through learning curves your entire life. You can use that experience with cold calling, too.

Choose a physical analogy

Think about the many times you've learned something that involved physical actions. How to cut lard into flour to make a perfect pie crust. How to swing a sand wedge, and where to place your feet to chip versus pitch. How to waltz or two-step, or serve a volley ball overhand—you get the idea.

We usually expect a learning curve when we learn a new physical action. We expect it to feel awkward and uncomfortable and we don't expect to be perfectly smooth or successful. We also know if we practice, stick with it—and get help as needed—we'll become comfortable and proficient.

So choose a physical analogy to remind yourself of the above. Choose something for which you remember the learning curve, that you now do pretty easily and well. Every time you wonder if you'll actually get good at cold calling, remember that analogy and dial the next call.

Make calls in a row

I've mentioned the importance of this many times now. While in the learning curve, making a number of calls in a row is vital.

Do not make a call, update CRM, look up an alternate word for "need," test it out by calling your co-worker, discuss whether that word or plain old "need" is better...

Do not make a call and then ponder how well it did or did not go.

Do not make a call and then discuss it with your manager—and try not to let her insist on that (have her talk to me).

Do not make a call, contemplate the value of standing up next time, check your favorite social media, then make another call.

Make a call. Make another call. Make another call. Make a bunch more calls until you have hit your dials goal. And then stop.

Determine basic CRM updates in advance

One of the things that gets in the way of making a bunch of calls in a row is dealing with CRM. The best way to prevent problems is to use a system built for calling, which unfortunately excludes most CRM. The second best way is to hone things down to as few items to update as possible. I recommend:

- Date of the call.

- "VM": indicates you left voicemail, or got voicemail and did not leave a message (if you're not leaving messages).

- "APPT": indicates an appointment was set. Show the date and time for it, too.

- Next call date, or apply tickler function, as applicable.

As for noting what the prospect said or other actions you may take; either use a notes field and type fast, or jot things down in a notebook. (Make more thorough notes in your follow-through period.)

Set dials goals you can hit

When people call me for help, I often discover they are not setting dials goals at all. Be sure to set them. Be sure to set dials goals you can reasonably hit, as well. Take the amount of time for your calling session into consideration, as well as how you feel about making calls.

If you stretch, stretch just a little

I know I've said you should not use stretch goals about eight billion times now—and that's true. However, many callers are prone to pushing themselves and think stretch goals are awesome. If this sounds like you, I'll say one more time that setting a goal you cannot hit sabotages the goal's benefits. If you insist on setting a stretch goal, make it a modest stretch. Missing a goal by one or two won't hurt as much as missing by ten or twenty.

Be yourself in your scripts

Remember that learning to write effective, natural-sounding scripts is a major contributor to success. It makes up about half of what people need to learn, so it's about half of the learning curve, too.

Your scripts are what will help you feel relaxed and confident. Writing the way you talk also provides a tool that helps you project confidence.

Don't let people tell you what you should say to make prospects react a certain way— that backfires.

If someone is helping with your scripts, have them focus on listening for whether you sound the way you normally do when feeling relaxed and confident.

Use a clear calling space

Even if you believe a messy desk is a sign of a creative mind, you probably know it's also distracting. Visual distractions hurt most in the learning curve.

See the tips in the next chapter about what to have in your calling space.

In addition: do not include a mirror. These do not actually remind us to smile, they create a distraction (as in gee, I need a haircut).

Let objections go for a while

We can only learn so much at once. To shorten your learning curve, focus on skills other than handling objections for a while. Use just Step 1 of the Call-Back Strategy, and let the rest go. Once you've got the basics down, add handling objections.

Take breaks

If your calling session covers several hours or more, take breaks every 45 minutes or so.

Do not let how you feel drive breaks because by the time you realize you're tired or thirsty or hungry, it's usually too late. That is, you've probably already made calls affected by feeling tired, etc. Some people set a timer to remind themselves to take a break.

STOP after you reach the dials goal

There are actually two ways to undermine the effect of using dials goals. One (stretch goals) has hopefully been put to bed.

The other thing that undermines the benefits of dials goals is making calls *past* the goal. This is especially harmful while in the learning curve.

When people have had an especially "good" final call that hits their goal, they often feel inspired to continue calling. They feel they're on a roll so they want to make the most of it.

When you go over the goal because you feel good, you're also teaching yourself to stop calling when things don't go so well. That will not develop one of the most important habits, which is:

- To give yourself enough opportunities
- To reach enough prospects
- So you have enough sales conversations
- So you have enough new business

It's also important to note that when the above habit is not developed, the learning curve is extended—possibly indefinitely—and so I repeat: Set dials goals you can hit. Stop after you reach the goal.

Know when to stop early, too

Sometimes nothing seems to go in our favor. Sometimes our personal life makes work life really tough. Sometimes we can't seem to string three words together. When you're having one of those times, take a break or stop calling for the day.

If you're having a tough time that may last a while, decrease your dials goal.

Use a reward system

Using a reward system is easy, and amazingly effective. Because too many callers discount such an unmacho approach to business, I'll provide background and details on using rewards.

My personal discovery of using a reward system occurred just as cafeterias began adding fresh-baked chocolate chip cookies to their menu. At that time, I and my colleagues spent every Monday making cold calls. I'd break for lunch. Go back to calling, start seriously dragging around 2 PM, and approximately one hour later the smell of cookies would waft down to our row of cubicles.

A buddy and I decided to commit to cranking out calls until fresh cookies were available, then we'd stop for the day and go have a couple cookies. There was something about knowing we'd enjoy a treat after calls that made it much easier to make those calls with high energy.

As importantly, soon after we started the above, both of us had better performance and were able to maintain that. I later realized it wasn't the promise of cookies, it was the immediate reward.

Why we need an immediate reward

Let's look at the two obvious rewards connected to cold calling. One is new business, but that often occurs days, weeks or months after making the calls. The other reward is setting appointments, but that doesn't happen with each call, or each and every set of calls.

Reaching a dials goal can be rewarding, but it's not tangible enough to make a significant impact for most people. Most of us need an immediate and more tangible reward—especially while in the learning curve—and it's easy to provide that for yourself.

Ineffective versus effective rewards

Things like enjoying a nice glass of wine at home are too far removed from calling, and will not be effective as rewards. "Not making more calls" is not a true reward, and using it that way will only reinforce negative feelings and habits.

Hitting the dials goal is not an effective reward by itself. Work tasks won't be effective, even if you find them relaxing or fun. Taking care of a task so you can leave work early won't be effective, either.

However, because effective rewards are also immediate, they are indeed things you have access to at or near your place of work. It needs to be something you can do in a relatively short period of time (e.g., 10 to 15 minutes), so it's relatively easy to fit into your day at the right time. Ideally, your reward also gets you up out of your chair and away from the phone for a bit. Here are some effective rewards your peers use:

- Get a fresh cup of tea or coffee, or a snack
- Take a walk to the corner and back—get some fresh air
- Step away from your desk and call or text a friend
- Hop onto your personal media sites for a few minutes
- Sit outside and people-watch
- Find a quiet spot and read or meditate for ten minutes
- If you have a home office, play with the dog or cat

Write the reward on your tracking sheet

When you get your copy of the tracking sheet, you'll see there's a place to write down the reward you'll take after you hit the dials goal. Writing the reward down in advance prompts you to think about it and choose in advance. This, in turn, sets the stage for immediate reward—which gives the reward its power.

Take your reward after completing the last call

Do not finish the last call, update CRM, send out emails, prepare for the sales appointments you set, and then take your reward. Do not finish the last call, tell your boss you're done and discuss things, and then take your reward.

Finish the last call, take a bathroom break if needed, and then take your reward. You may be amazed at the difference adding this habit makes.

How long will the learning curve last?

Before I answer that question, a definition may be important. When we say something is "learned," we mean we can access the skills when we want, carry them out fairly well, and feel pretty comfortable doing that. So how long does it take to get to this point?

For people making calls for at least one hour every work day, it tends to take a couple weeks to complete the learning curve and move into refining their approach.

For people making calls a couple times a week, it tends to take four to six weeks.

Consider using a ramp-up period

If you have reason to believe your learning curve will be steep, you may want to invest time upfront to cover it. For example:

- Instead of calling once a week for several months
- Block and schedule calling and related tasks on a daily or twice-weekly basis.

Using that kind of ramp-up period often shortens the learning curve.

Next

Calling is a marketing tool that's effective for a broad range of situations, industries, and so on. The next chapter provides tips for putting cold calling to work whenever you want to, and for almost any purpose.

There are also tips to apply while in the learning curve, so be sure to read the chapter before you get started.

Using Calling Whenever You Want

MOST PEOPLE WHO read this book do not make calls all day, every day. Some do, but most readers want to use what they have learned on an as-needed basis. They're calling a couple/few times a week, every couple weeks, or may have a calling campaign several times a year.

This chapter is written for those readers, including people who need to quickly refresh good habits and apply best practices. Those of who use calling all day (or close to that) will find a lot of this chapter will work for you, too. However, you're also invited to contact me to get specific tips for daily calling.

Remember to use best practices

The above headline could also be "Don't get lazy." The more we become accustomed to cold calling, the more likely we are to try to cut corners or wing it. (Even I have made this mistake.)

That can hurt results, especially if you're calling just 20 prospects instead of 200. By the time you realize you should back up and get some tools in place, you may have completed half of your dials. So don't let things get that far—use the best practices described below.

Create scripts and use them

Have your scripts out and ready for reference:

- You need a Contact/Prospect script.

- You may need a Gatekeeper script; however experienced callers can often use the Contact/Prospect script because the content is so similar.

- You need your objections-handling reference. This should show the call-back strategy at the top because it will be used most often.

- Leaving voicemail? Then you need that script, too.

Practice?

If it's been a while since you made calls, or if you feel nervous about calling these particular prospects, practice each script a little bit. (See and apply the tips about over-thinking it, too.)

Block time, and schedule in your calendar

- Block time for preparation; which includes preparing your scripts, doing any research, and warming up.

- Block time for calling. Make sure it's enough time to hit your dials goal and take any breaks.

- Block time for follow through.

- Include time to take a reward. Use time at the end of your calling block, or at the beginning of follow through if that's scheduled right after calling.

Before you begin: clear your space

Clear your calling space so it's easier to focus. You should have the just following:

- All scripts on paper (printed, that is)

- Tracking sheet(s) on paper

- CRM or list on screen, or list on paper

- Notebook for quick notes (recommended)

- Beverage

- Phone

The above also improves calling results

Using the above guideline is about more than a tidy desk. Here's the scoop:

Our brains do better with printed material, so scripts on paper are more effective than on a screen.

Marking calls off on the tracking sheet has <u>far</u> stronger benefits than clicking a mouse or keyboard to count them.

However, most of us use software to manage lists, and sometimes to dial, so having that on screen often works best.

Avoid multi-tasking

Multi-tasking hurts occasional callers more than those who call daily. Turn off pop-ups and dingers, mobile phones, etc. Try to prevent coworkers from trying to talk to you, too.

Set and use dials goals

Remember laziness can bite you—so can being cocky. Do not skip the best practice of setting dials goals, and set goals you can hit.

Choose and use a reward

The reward system is very helpful: period. Rather than waiting to see if you need it, choose a reward ahead of time and apply it.

Prepare and use a tracking sheet

(Contact me to get a tracking sheet and instructions.) Use the tracking sheet to note the dials goal, reward, and everything else described in the previous chapter. This serves to remind you of many best practices on one sheet of paper.

Use the tracking sheet as you call. Marking calls off as you call will be more beneficial than you may imagine. Collecting the data will be, too, even though it will take a while to collect enough to analyze.

Energy waning as you call?

Most of us get tired after calling for 45 minutes or so. Set things up so you can take breaks. Use an alarm-reminder if needed.

Some people find taking breaks every 30 minutes is better, especially when in the learning curve or if it's been a while since they used cold calling.

Not enough sales conversations?

The benefits of repetition can weaken if we're not calling often enough. If you're calling less frequently than once a month and do not have enough sales conversations, try calling more often (potentially also using smaller dials goals).

If you're calling more often than monthly and don't have enough sales conversations, contact me for help.

Feeling bored?

You probably need new scripts. Start over, beginning with objectives.

If you're stuck for content, stay away from what's on websites and marketing collateral. Focus instead on what you like about the products or services and/or stories your customers have shared.

Write as if you're explaining things to a friend—someone with whom you feel relaxed and self-confident—and use simple wording. Avoid industry jargon.

Beware over-thinking

Knowledge of the nuances of consultative calling can be a nifty procrastination device. Here are tips for avoiding problems:

- When writing scripts, limit re-writes to three.

  After a third re-write; pick up the phone and use the script, or start all over (beginning with clarifying your objective for the calls).

- Do not record yourself, except to test the length of your voicemail message.

- Do not analyze each call.

- Remember that you need a large enough pool of data for contact rate guidelines and statistical analysis to be realistic.

  You need 100 or more dials that took place within a reasonable short period of time (e.g., over a couple weeks or less, not over six months).

Above all, be yourself!

Talk about the products and services you believe in. Use your own regular way of talking. Be more serious if you're more serious, or use humor if that's who you are.

And remember: Your goal is not to overcome every single challenge that comes your way, your goal is to work with every opportunity.

Next: Go Make Some Good Mistakes

To apply what's been covered in this book you need to draft some scripts, get a list together, set a dials goal, prepare a tracking sheet, get your tools and calling space ready...

And then pick up the phone and make a bunch of calls.

Be yourself, give it some time, and reach out for help as needed—I'm here for you.

In Closing...the Lines are Open

WAY BACK WHEN I had my first job that required serious dedication to cold calling, things did not start well. Compared to my colleagues, I was at the bottom of the heap. The way, way bottom.

I was fortunate to have an excellent sales manager—known to his team as "Murphy"—who was a good coach and had clear standards for the number of calls we were to make.

Frankly, he could be downright scary if we did something to piss him off. I did not want to do that, and also had a bit of a crush—I wanted his praise. And so when Murphy told us we must make 250 dials every Monday, I did. "It ain't an option," he'd say. (Woe to those who did not make the dials, but that's not the point of this story.)

In addition to weekly team meetings, Murphy held weekly meetings with each of us to go over calling and sales. There was no chit-chat when I sat down for my one-on-one, he'd jump right in and ask how many dials I had made. At first my response was, "250, *but*" and then I'd try to add that I didn't have many appointments or sales. Murphy would interrupt, tell me I was doing well with dials, and curtly dismiss me.

That went on for a while: I sat at the very bottom of the sales performance report, making calls so at least I wouldn't get yelled at. And then I had more appointments...and more. And then I had more and more sales conversations. And then I led our group in sales, and then the division, and then the whole group company-wide, and pretty much stayed at the top or in the top five.

Thanks to heeding my smart, supportive, scary sales manager, I learned that if I make enough dials, I'll reach enough people, to have enough opportunities to have enough sales conversations, to have enough sales.

That knowledge and experience has served me well ever since; from later sales positions, to selling my own company's services. I hope this book helps you enjoy similar value.

To help you get there, you're welcome to contact me to get help with scripts, strategy, butt-kicking, and encouragement. Every reader gets some free coaching. See savageandgreene.com for contact information.

Tracking Sheet & Reward System

(Partial sample - contact Savage and Greene for full Sheet)

Name: _____

Day of week: _____

List/Prospect type: _____

Date: _____

Time of day: _____

Objective: _____

Reward: _____

Dials goal: _____

Dials	Got Voicemail	Connect	Next Step	NAP
Including wrong numbers, fax, disconnected, etc	☐ Not leaving messages	With live human	e.g. Sales appt set got contact info	Use when you absolutely will not call again
1 2 3 4 5 6 7 8 9 10	1 2 3 4 5 6 7 8 9 10	1 2 3 4 5 6 7 8 9 10	1 2 3 4 5 6 7 8 9 10	1 2 3 4 5 6 7 8 9 10
1 2 3 4 5 6 7 8 9 20	1 2 3 4 5 6 7 8 9 20	1 2 3 4 5 6 7 8 9 20	1 2 3 4 5 6 7 8 9 20	1 2 3 4 5 6 7 8 9 20
1 2 3 4 5 6 7 8 9 30	1 2 3 4 5 6 7 8 9 30	1 2 3 4 5 6 7 8 9 30	1 2 3 4 5 6 7 8 9 30	1 2 3 4 5 6 7 8 9 30
1 2 3 4 5 6 7 8 9 40	1 2 3 4 5 6 7 8 9 40	1 2 3 4 5 6 7 8 9 40	1 2 3 4 5 6 7 8 9 40	1 2 3 4 5 6 7 8 9 40
1 2 3 4 5 6 7 8 9 50	1 2 3 4 5 6 7 8 9 50	1 2 3 4 5 6 7 8 9 50	1 2 3 4 5 6 7 8 9 50	1 2 3 4 5 6 7 8 9 50
1 2 3 4 5 6 7 8 9 60	1 2 3 4 5 6 7 8 9 60	1 2 3 4 5 6 7 8 9 60	1 2 3 4 5 6 7 8 9 60	1 2 3 4 5 6 7 8 9 60
% of dials	% of dials	% of dials	% of connect	% of dials or connect

Readers are free to use this version; however, I encourage you to contact me for a full-size sheet with tips & instructions

Training, Speaking
& Instructional Design Services

The story this book opens with is true—and the training workshop came first. Every time I delivered the program, participants and their bosses told me I should write a book. One summer, I let the ya-ya to be a 'real' writer take hold and did just that. However, it's my work as a sales performance expert and trainer that continues to inform each edition.

Training programs teach consultative cold calling and selling skills, as well as customer service skills. Most are customized to suit each client, and can be delivered via classroom or webinar. Train-the-trainer is available, as is my cadre of certified trainers.

Speaking programs focus on prospecting and selling topics. Whether a keynote or break-out session, programs use concrete examples and pragmatic tips to ensure attendees get full value from their time and attention.

Back in 1966, when Mom's reading of *Harriet the Spy* opened my eyes to the craft of writing, I had no idea of the shapes and forms writing can take. My horizons and skills expanded since then, and I do quite a bit of instructional design. Deliverables and expertise include comprehensive training curriculum, single and unique programs, as well as policy and procedure references.

See SavageAndGreene.com for insight into substance and style, and for articles mentioned in this book.

Artist Credits

I am in awe of artists who create typefaces and fonts. In this print version:

Cover title and chapter headings use Museo Slab
Subtitles use Century Gothic
Main text uses Linux Libertine

I am equally in awe of the artist who created this edition's cover:

James Ketsdever and the amazing Sara Waters—both powering the Sara Waters Design Group.

37502793R00133

Made in the USA
Middletown, DE
27 February 2019